CONSCIOUS
MARRIAGE

CONSCIOUS
Marriage

FROM CHEMISTRY TO COMMUNICATION

JOHN C. LUCAS

THE CROSSING PRESS
FREEDOM, CALIFORNIA

To my daughter, Carmen

Copyright © 1998 by John C. Lucas
Cover design by Tara M. Eoff
Printed in the U.S.A.

First published in 1997 by Simon & Schuster Australia

For information on bulk purchases or group discounts for this and other Crossing Press titles, please contact our Special Sales Manager at 800-777-1048 x214.

Visit our Web site on the Internet: www.crossingpress.com

Library of Congress Cataloging-in-Publication Data
Lucas, John C. (John Clifton)
   Conscious marriage: from chemistry to communication / by John C. Lucas.
      p. cm.
   Originally published: Simon & Schuster Australia, 1997.
   Includes index.
   ISBN 0-89594-915-6 (pbk.)
   1. Marriage. 2. Communication in marriage. 3. Man-woman relationships. I. Title.
HQ734.L7676   1998
306.81--dc21   98-5021
                                                         CIP

CONTENTS

PREFACE:
WELCOME TO THE TWENTY-FIRST CENTURY

For relationships, moving toward the new millennium means facing the past, the present, as well as the future — and distinguishing between what didn't work, what isn't working and what will.

Relationship is a charged issue. We have almost all had failures, sometimes quite painful ones. Reading about how a relationship should develop to be functional, or even how a relationship could become an ideal, may make you feel inadequate or bring up unresolved feelings from the past.

But this is part of the learning — and healing — process. I have experienced this process from both chairs: that of the therapist and the client. I failed in an embarrassing number of relationships. I have been through a divorce, though mercifully one in which no children were involved. I have made most of the mistakes possible. And I've hung in there. I learned the hard way. For the past twelve years I have been in a growing relationship, ten of them in a committed marriage.

The perspective of *Conscious Marriage* is one point of view — by no means the only one. It is my point of view based on twenty-five years of personal and professional experience. After many years (too many!) I began to notice what actually worked in other couples' relationships and in my own: what allowed growth to occur, what course that growth took, and what the ideal relationship would be like. I have taken what I have observed about others' relationships, my own experience of them, and what I have learned, and constructed a theoretical model of relationship. A theory is based on supposition, it is hypothetical. It is not a law; it does not say how it is, but how it may be. However, I would not have written this book had I not been persuaded of what it takes to make a relationship work.

The subtitle of this book helpfully offers a suggestion about what the conscious marriage model is for — to make marriage work. The idea is that couples can use this approach to improve the effectiveness of their own relationship, to move toward fulfilment together.

The first step is to understand what a conscious marriage is all about. A helpful approach to adopt when venturing into new territory is to go in there with and open mind. Twenty years ago I began the training for crisis counsellors in a particular helping model by encouraging them to take on the model's viewpoint. This involved them suspending their preconceptions and judgments, setting aside their personal theories or what they had previously learned, for the duration of the training so as to be able to understand the model they were being taught. The theory being that to use a tool, you first have to pick it up — and this takes an open hand. After the training, prospective counsellors could evaluate what they had learned and apply what seemed worthwhile to them. I would encourage you to adopt this strategy with the model of relationship presented in the following chapters. Still, many of the terms used will unavoidably trigger associations to other systems, other models, other therapeutic theories. The word 'marriage' itself carries heavy baggage, as do 'commitment', 'pragmatic' and 'chemistry' for that matter. These terms have specific meanings as used in the context of this model. There may be no new word for marriage, but there can be a new marriage — one based on a conscious, committed relationship. Throughout this book I have used the term marriage to define a committed, sexually exclusive relationship.

There have been some positive changes affecting relationships and marriage in the last generation. Increased equality between women and men is a notable example. This change has dented the old authoritarian structure between husband and wife and, though positive, makes relationships even more challenging. There have also been 'new developments', like 'serial relationships', which have further destabilised marriage. 'Serial relationships' promised liberation from the bonds of a stagnant situation and the opportunity for personal growth, but have frequently kept its adherents on a treadmill. If you are happy in your series of relationships, or if the traditional model of marriage is what you really want, conscious marriage is probably not for you. The view expressed in this book is that neither approach has done the job for couples: conventional marriage to my mind is virtually synonymous with dysfunction; and 'serial relationships', while offering the well-deserved chance to try again, all too often become a licence for repeated failure. While the breakdown of the conventional form of marriage has given rise to variations on a theme, I believe that theme for the most part has been one of marriage destructuring. And the products of destructuring are unstable forms of relationship. While often springing from a sincere motivation for improvement, they have just as frequently failed to work. What is needed now is conscious restructuring to achieve an effective framework for marriage.

Conscious Marriage suggests restructuring relationship along pragmatic lines, in a way that works. It has worked for me and my wife, and various aspects of the model have worked for many couples. I believe that virtually any functional relationship will bear recognisable similarities to the conscious marriage model. Conscious marriage offers couples who wish to go beyond the old model of marriage and the 'new developments' in relationship the opportunity to have a truly fulfilling marriage. Conscious attention on the growth of their relationship, I am convinced, will help couples to move out of the dark ages and into a brighter future for their marriage.

1 A NEW MODEL FOR MAKING MARRIAGE WORK

There is nothing more difficult to take in hand, more perilous

to conduct or more uncertain in its success than to take the

lead in the introduction of a new order of things.

Niccolo Machiavelli

Relationships come and go, work or do not work, and grow or end — almost randomly it seems sometimes. Technology is at a premium in today's world, but marriage is cheap. As thoroughly as hard science has succeeded in explaining the workings of the physical world, social science has failed to give couples an appropriate 'technology' to make marriage work.

The idea of making marriage work may seem to conflict with how relationships should be — magical and romantic. Unfortunately, there is a frog in every prince and a pea under every princess just waiting to foul up fairytale relationships. But, if couples can learn how to make the magic themselves, then they will be able to keep their relationship's promise — the creation of a better life together.

THE KEY TO MAKING MARRIAGE WORK

Many couples are looking for a way to succeed in their relationship. They want more out of marriage than a habitual arrangement; and they have not given up on making marriage work. Yet often in spite of monumentous efforts to achieve success, things fall apart. What is required is a new perspective, a new way of seeing marriage. Changing the way we regard marriage is the first step on a conscious journey to fulfilment in relationship.

What would 'a new order of things' for marriage look like? What makes a marriage work? How can a couple in love support the growth of their relationship? What brings a couple together, holds them together and keeps them together?

The key is effective relationship: *an effective marriage is based on an effective relationship.* To be involved in a marriage that works means more than avoiding dysfunction and divorce; it demands choosing to participate in the development of a healthy relationship. By definition a 'new order' for marriage would be one designed to guide growth within relationship. Only an effective relationship can support a marriage and make it really work — it may not be a fairytale, but it will have its own magic . . . the synergistic power of marriage.

THE PROMISE OF SYNERGISTIC MARRIAGE

When at its best, marriage is synergistic: the action of the whole accomplishes more than the partners could separately. The excitement of relating positively, of sexual satisfaction, and of achieving success in marriage and in life flow from this synergy. A true union of two individuals comes alive as an entity when they are fully involved in the life of their relationship. The couple move with purpose and can seem to work wonders. Two people who have fallen in love know this magical power — anything seems possible to them. The action of synergy promises to accomplish no less than marital fulfilment.

GROWTH, CHOICE AND RESPONSIBILITY

The secret to having a good relationship is growth. If a relationship does not grow, it will stagnate. No couple will ever be perfect, but growth moves them in the right direction. When the challenges come — and they always do — an effective relationship is one that grows through them.

Growth is a process. A growing relationship is a living, changing creation. For a couple, growth means moving forward together. As their relationship grows, it develops, it improves. Over time the couple become closer, more committed, and happier together.

A couple must learn how to keep their relationship growing — it does not just happen. Relationship is often effortless in the beginning, but later wilful efforts will at times become necessary.

Romance taps the power of synergy, and continuing growth channels it into the development of an effective relationship. Simply stated, a relationship that grows, works. Making a marriage work means making and keeping the relationship growing, dynamic and, in this way, alive.

Relationship is based on choice. Two individuals exercising their free will to be in contact have a relationship. If the element of choice is not present, there is no relationship. A couple who have not chosen to be together live parallel lives; they may be together physically but not psychologically. On the other hand, a couple who have actually chosen to be in a relationship have created a connection to one another. This is a powerful occurrence. An inexhaustible potential flows from the free and conscious connection between two people. It is the magic. Each of their lives becomes more than it ever could be alone. This is what couples are after in relationship.

Falling in love brings the power of synergy to a couple's life together, but often they don't know how to sustain it. By understanding how choice operates in relationships, a couple can get a handle on the dynamic process in which they are involved and actively direct it towards happiness.

The basic choice each partner has is to relate to the other or not. This is such a fundamental fact that it can be easily overlooked. Being conscious of the choice to relate can empower you to influence the outcome of your relationship. But the choice to relate to your partner is not a one-off happening that, once made, holds forever. It is an on-going reality affecting every interchange between a couple and every stage of their relationship. A couple who choose to relate to each other feel right about being together. They glow, they click, it all happens for them. If they are not choosing to relate, they experience repeated insurmountable obstacles that seem external, but are all really based on their fundamental choice.

The implications of choice stretch across the whole spectrum of a couple's life together, and this will show up throughout the following chapters. How a couple choose to treat each other, how they handle differences, value commitment, how well they communicate and cooperate, and how they deal with the issue of choice in their sex life, are all important areas in which choice becomes a tool for growth. The principle underlying all these areas is the same: *a couple has the power to choose to improve their relationship.* This is the single most important piece of information for any couple to have. For their success, for their happiness together, for the fulfilment of their marriage, knowing that they *can* make their marriage work is an invaluable and indispensable tool. Sometimes it will not seem possible, but it is if couples work together. It is not enough for just one partner to try; it is not possible for one individual to make a relationship work. However, if two individuals continue to choose to relate, all manner of obstacles can be overcome. The couple will keep their connection alive, they will make their own magic.

With the choice to relate comes the responsibility to continue improving the relationship. A couple who have connected have a responsibility to each other to maintain and deepen their contact. To some degree this will proceed of its own accord, but from time to time the couple will need to consciously exercise their choice to keep the connection viable. Responsibility sustains a couple's growth.

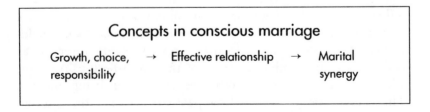

Concepts in conscious marriage

Growth, choice,   →   Effective relationship   →   Marital
responsibility   synergy

BEYOND YESTERDAY AND TODAY

These days more than a little pessimism surrounds the institution of marriage. In the last thirty years marriage has earned its bad reputation from a skyrocketing divorce rate, valid criticism from the women's movement and an increasingly clear failure to provide a workable framework for intimate relationships.

Perhaps it is the cycle of change that has affected the viability of marriage. The social revolution of the 1960s overtly confronted conventional marriage with its weaknesses. The social facade, the sexual avoidance, and the insular out-of-touch quality of post-war marriage could not stand up under the scrutiny. The institution of marriage has been in a destructuring phase for decades since. While the divorce rate has more than doubled, marriage has not yet found a new configuration. Experiments such as 'open marriage' in the 1970s, the 'DINKS' (double income no kids) of the 1980s, and the growing trend towards 'serial relationships' spanning the last three decades have largely failed. Marriage has not reintegrated into a workable pattern that provides challenge and satisfaction to couples and serves the function of childrearing.

This breakdown has occurred largely because in traditional marriage too little attention was paid to the fundamental relationship. In conventional marriage, authority rested with the husband, sexuality was not openly discussed, and both partners — especially the wife — were called upon to sacrifice their individual needs for those of the marriage. A suppressive style of relating, poor communication and sexual avoidance were the norm. The importance of growth was not understood; the centrality of choice was not acknowledged; and responsibility meant avoiding divorce at all costs.

A whole generation has now come of age knowing, or at least suspecting, that traditional marriage is failing. As well, starting in the 1960s, many women and men have left their marriages, motivated by a sincere wish to better their relationship lives. Out of frustration with the old form, or in their urge to grow beyond it, many young people as well as relationship veterans have countered traditional marriage by choosing not to marry or have children, or to have children without being married. In what might be termed the counter-traditional approach, the poles were reversed. Non-communication in traditional marriage was replaced by confrontation, sexual avoidance was replaced by irresponsibility, male dominance was replaced by a power struggle, emphasis on sacrifice for the marriage's sake was replaced by self-indulgence, and the suppressive style of relating remained the same. Replacing traditional patterns of relating that have proved dysfunctional with equally, or even more, dysfunctional counter-traditional ones has not provided couples with a realistic alternative to conventional marriage.

For a generation the traditional and counter-traditional approaches have run a kind of competition against each other — without a winner. In the 1990s a new form of marriage may finally be emerging — one that will take marriage into the twenty-first century. Couples whose relationships are working today have brought the best elements of both approaches together. The counter-traditional model's emphasis on communication, personal growth, and freedom complements the traditional model's characteristic commitment, responsibility and stability. The new model actually goes beyond the old models because it stresses relationship. By making conscious what may be trying to happen spontaneously in relationship, a couple can actively participate in building a happy marriage.

Conscious marriage

Falling in love and beginning a relationship may be compared to taking a rowboat out into a steadily flowing river on a sunny day. There are two schools of thought on how to make the most of the voyage. The first approach is to ship the oars, lean back, float down the river and enjoy. The other approach is to grasp the oars solidly, heave to, and row. The advantages and disadvantages of both are fairly clear. The first promises freedom, spontaneity and pleasure; the second offers a sense of control, direction and involvement.

However, when the boat hits the rapids waiting just around the bend, the dozing floater may be dumped in the drink and lose all, while the rower can safely navigate through the obstacles. Conversely, while the floater will appreciate the beauty of the journey, the rower preoccupied with duty may miss it altogether.

In an ideal world the river would flow on to the sea unobstructed and the first approach would work splendidly. The river of the real world, however, has bends, jagged rocks, stagnant backwaters, rapids and even the occasional waterfall. To apply the carefree philosophy in this environment would be foolhardy. Using the wilful approach, a couple could run the rapids avoiding the rocks, portage around the falls, row out of the still backwaters and quite thoroughly miss the joy and wonder of it all. Neither school of thought alone is enough to make a relationship work.

The trick is to pay attention, to know when to let go and drift, and when to take up the oars and row. A couple may adopt this third approach, integrating the best features of both philosophies while avoiding their disadvantages. *The key to doing this is for the couple to keep their attention on the relationship.* This is neither an active nor a passive method but a conscious one. By placing your attention on the relationship you notice when wilful activity is appropriate and when letting go is realistic. This conscious approach is suggested for making marriage work: *conscious marriage.*

Paying attention to a relationship also implies knowing where it is going. Relationship has a course with discernible stages — landmarks — along the way and a direction. Many variations of a relationship's course are possible. An informed couple can consciously make their own way instead of drifting off-course, or onto one that is a dead end.

By understanding relationship, by acknowledging that growth is the secret of a healthy relationship, and by knowing the importance of choice in an effective relationship, a couple can consciously support their own marriage. Being aware of the developmental course of a relationship allows a couple to mark their progress, anticipate difficulties and keep the final goal in sight as they attend to the give and take of their life together. By using the approach of conscious marriage, they will know when and how to act and when to relax to keep the relationship on course.

Know-how is supportive in relationship, but in conscious marriage success ultimately hinges on responsibility. If only one partner is choosing to improve the relationship, the other is failing in his or her responsibility. 'Response ability' may be a helpful way to think of it: two people who have their attention on their relationship, have their attention on one another, and respond to each other in a way that promotes growth. Responding to the other is a manifestation of love. It powers the relationship forward through the various stages. It overcomes the forces pulling a couple apart.

Conscious marriage presents a couple with a great opportunity and a great challenge. In this book, you will be introduced to a series of straightforward techniques that can prevent or solve problems that usually come up in the course of a couple's life together. Ethics in relating, goals identification, choice in commitment, communication techniques and a method for building consensus are the tools which can smooth the course of a relationship's development.

Frankly, it *is* perilous to try to have an effective relationship. Inevitably, problems will come up — sometimes hairy ones. There will be repeated ups and downs. Just when it seems things are finally going smoothly, something else will unexpectedly go wrong. However, forewarned is forearmed.

Conscious marriage is for couples who seriously want their relationship to work and are willing to do what is necessary to make it do so. For couples who want to go beyond the traditional and counter-traditional models of marriage to a new level of marital synergy, *conscious* marriage is the key. That so many couples have tried and failed in their relationships, that so many are struggling against forces they do not fully understand, shows that being in an effective relationship is not easy. Conscious marriage shows that it *is* possible.

Thinkers, doers, lovers and conscious marriage

For some people, just knowing the relevant information is enough to help them avoid the serious obstacles of relationship. These are primarily thinking individuals. They are interested in data, concepts and knowledge. Thinkers can drive their partners to distraction with abstraction. Others are less interested in the theory but, given a technique based on it, will succeed through sheer industry. These are the doers. They like the action of relating. Doers may wear their partners out with constant activity. Still another type of person relies on love to conquer all. This devotional type, the lover, will naturally keep his or her attention on the relationship and often do the right thing at the right time. Sometimes lovers demand more attention — or give more attention — than their partners can handle. The lover may eschew both theory and practice and still succeed, or may get carried away by the passion of it all. Being exposed to the relevant knowledge and techniques may help them to stay on track. Everyone, of whatever type or combination of types, will experience difficulties from time to time, and probably find knowledge and practice helpful to fall back on.

These types are not meant to force anyone into a mould. Everyone really has features of each type, although one is usually predominant.

Some sections of this book may be more useful to the thinkers, the doers or the lovers. The concepts involved in making marriage work would probably appeal more to a knowledge-oriented type. An action-oriented individual will probably want to do the techniques, and by incessantly doing them may alienate a knowledge-oriented partner (the devotional type would go along out of love). A devotional type may leave this book on the shelf and have a satisfying relationship or another disaster. By being sensitive to your own interests in this respect and to your partners, you can make optimal use of the model of conscious marriage.

2 DEVELOPING AN EFFECTIVE RELATIONSHIP

To understand something is to be delivered from it.

Spinoza

If a couple do not take responsibility for improving their relationship, things can start to come unglued and problems build up. Often couples just drift. Sometimes they collide violently. The romantic dream can too easily turn into a nightmare if a couple neglect their relationship. When the magic is gone, a couple's life can become tantamount to hell itself: it may be a noisy hell or a very quiet one.

The more things change for marriage, it seems, the more they stay the same. Too many marriages continue to be violent, chaotic and abusive, or aimless, uncommitted and competitive. Too few relationships grow and develop intimacy, effective communication and cooperation, or are able to balance the individual partners' needs with those of the union. In short, too many marriages still become what they should not, too few marriages become what they could.

Get away closer!

His dark good looks pulled her closer. His self-satisfied inability to grasp anyone else's point of view pushed her away. His brilliant intellect and refined artistic sensibility tugged at her own, but his commitment phobia raised her warning antenna. How could he be so articulate and so intractable at the same time? He didn't understand why he kept getting mixed messages from her.

Taking up the challenge of relationship means facing up to an inescapable reality, which we will explore in the next section.

PERSONAL GROWTH FOR COUPLES

As surely as women and men are driven into contact by powerful forces, so are they driven apart by competing, often time-lagged, forces. These countervailing energies that propel partners to almost constant variations of 'get away closer' are instinctual, emotional and mental in nature.

The reproductive instinct, the desire to love and be loved, and the idea of finding a better life in relationship pull couples together. Other forces destructive to relationship create obstacles, which, if not overcome, pull couples apart. Some of the common psychological obstacles couples face are abusive patterns of relating, the subconscious mind's tendency to subvert their conscious intentions, lack of commitment, dysfunctional communication patterns and competitiveness.

Everyone encounters barriers in relationship — they need not be the source of blame and recrimination between the sexes. Virtually everyone would like to have a good relationship, and if it was easy, everyone would. A couple must work together, and hard at that, to keep their relationship growing.

Only during the last thirty years, a tiny span in the totality of human history, has the idea of 'working on a relationship' become widespread. It is difficult to imagine a couple from a thousand or even a hundred years ago intentionally taking steps to improve their relationship. Historically a relationship was considered effective if both partners survived danger, illness and the elements long enough to reproduce. If a woman lived through childbirth it was an added blessing.

The concept of relationship and what to expect of it has evolved since the 1960s with the growth of the personal development movement. Many ideas, techniques and practices that had been the exclusive province of psychotherapy were generalised to help people deal with issues themselves, and many benefited from personal growth. Nonetheless, the aspirations fostered by the quest for personal growth have often outstripped couples' ability to overcome the obstacles to effective relationship — obstacles that would not have been considered problematic in the past. These days a proliferation of expectations surrounds relationship. In this new era couples have come to expect a fulfilling one. Fulfilment is possible in marriage, both individually and as a union . . . but first couples have to face up to their problems.

A couple in a conscious marriage acknowledge the forces that threaten the development of an effective relationship, take responsibility for improving their relationship, and confront and deal with its problems. Working with couples' problems has traditionally been the domain of counselling and psychotherapy, depending on the severity of the problems and the personal resources of the couple. *Conscious marriage puts the power to succeed in their relationship in the couple's hands.* The map of relationship's development outlined in this chapter and the next offers an alternative to getting professional help with relationship problems: personal growth for couples. In a conscious marriage a couple can get a handle on practical solutions themselves. Based on the knowledge of what helps a relationship develop, they can strengthen the forces holding their relationship together, while redirecting and healing the forces breaking it apart. Couples can grow despite obstacles by exercising their choice to improve their relationship.

In any marriage, a couple will hit barriers. Perhaps they have a problem communicating: every time they try to discuss an important topic, they have an argument. Debilitating problems will occur in a relationship unless the barriers are overcome. In this case, unless the couple learn how to communicate, their marriage will become more and more dysfunctional. *A couple's problems are often a manifestation of the arrested growth of their relationship.*

Using the model of conscious marriage, a couple support the process of growth in their relationship. They keep their attention on the relationship; they work on their relationship to solve problems when they hit barriers. For example, faced with an important decision — whether to buy a new house — the couple would realise that discussing the topic is important *for their relationship*. If they hit a barrier — an argument — they would immediately recognise the trouble as a communication problem and then quickly confront it. In the event that they couldn't stop interrupting each other, they could take a break or they might set a kitchen timer every five minutes to help them take turns speaking. Through months and years of dealing with every variation of how communication can malfunction between them, a couple in a conscious marriage are able to ensure that effective communication keeps their relationship growing.

Personal growth for couples

1. A couple work on their relationship.
2. They hit a barrier.
3. A problem stops the relationship's growth.
4. The couple confront the problem, put the missing factor in place, and growth continues.

The ability to communicate effectively is a vital tool for establishing, maintaining, and promoting relationship: it is one of the factors that makes marriage work. Altogether there are five crucial components that need to be present if a relationship is to succeed.

THE FIVE CS OF DEVELOPING AN EFFECTIVE RELATIONSHIP

Instead of just taking their chances, if a couple know what is coming and how to grow on through it, they can prevent or solve problems instead of being threatened or dragged down by them. There are Five Cs of developing an effective relationship. If they appear, the relationship will flourish; if they do not, growth will be interrupted and the relationship will stall. The Five Cs help a couple to understand how growth optimally proceeds and where and how it may be stopped. Each factor is crucial at a particular stage in the life of their relationship, and each appears as a couple successfully confront the challenges the relationship brings their way.

A couple who know about the Five Cs have an advantage in making their relationship work: they have a map. With it they can identify where they are and where they are going, what causes problems and how to solve them. The Five Cs of developing an effective relationship are like markers in the life of a relationship; they mark the way for couples to success.

When all the Five Cs are put into place, barriers are overcome and synergy reaches its full power in a conscious marriage.

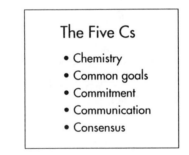

The Five Cs

- Chemistry
- Common goals
- Commitment
- Communication
- Consensus

Chemistry

If there is no *chemistry* from the point of that first glance, the probability of a relationship coming to life is greatly diminished. 'Chemistry' denotes interest, attraction, including sexual attraction, and those biochemical changes that can make even the most sober among us appear patently foolish. Chemistry precedes romance; it defines the edge of the precipice of falling in love. When there is chemistry between two people, there is a desire to know more about the other, to be in the physical presence of the other and to open oneself to that other. In the first stage of a relationship, chemistry is a high qualification for a relationship's eventual workability.

Chemistry is further discussed in Chapter 4.

Common goals

In relationship's second stage, for two individuals to develop their attraction into a meaningful bond, *common goals* prominently come into play. The couple may never notice this factor or its absence — nevertheless, its presence (or absence) foretells the relationship's future. After their first meeting, a couple may be off happily whacking a tennis ball back and forth, or they may find themselves sitting in front of a television fifteen years later wondering what happened. For a relationship to be truly compatible, partners must have a shared direction in life. If not, what are they doing together? Sharing common goals is essential to the development of a successful relationship because it bonds a couple together. As a relationship grows and matures, the couple learn to share their lives with each other.

The importance of common goals is further discussed in Chapter 5.

Commitment

Even with chemistry and common goals, in the third stage a relationship will lose its cohesion without *commitment*. An effective relationship depends on an enduring commitment. Commitment can be intimidating to an individual and to a couple. It is making a choice that, if changed, could hurt the individual and undermine a couple's life together. Many men and women simply go in the opposite direction when this topic comes up. Commitment threatens to swallow up the self in a union of unknown value. It is a risk, it is an act of faith, it is a sacrifice — it drives the ego crazy.

Commitment also happens to pave the way to a kind of satisfaction that a relationship lacking it will never have. A relationship can turn into a conscious marriage with a conscious commitment. Making a commitment means a couple choose to devote their energies to the sustenance of the relationship over time: not until a crisis is raging, not until the next attraction presents itself and also not necessarily until death does them part. To commit to one course of action means that involvement in other possibilities is relinquished. 'Forsaking all others' it is termed in the marriage ceremony. In this respect, commitment is a sacrifice. Ironically, while commitment may seem to lead to restricting confinement, in the context of a growing relationship it can lead to freedom.

Commitment is further discussed in Chapter 6.

Communication

More relationships probably fail because of poor *communication* than any other reason. In the fourth stage of relationship, good communication makes a marriage functional; poor communication makes it dysfunctional. While communication is not the only factor essential for a relationship to be effective, its crucial value must be acknowledged. From beginning to end, day in and day out, all night long on occasion, communication occurring is the marriage working. The inability to communicate lies at the root of many relationship problems. A working ability to express themselves verbally, when brought to bear with care and persistence, will undercut problems and open the contact between a couple. The marriage will deepen, and success will be added to success if the partners can effectively communicate.

Communication, its importance and how to do it effectively, is further discussed in Chapter 7.

Consensus

Cooperation is the hallmark of a mature relationship; *consensus* between a couple makes it possible. Consensual decision making gives rise to cooperative efforts by partners, and becomes the standard operating procedure in an effective marriage. In consensus both partners choose a course of action, thereby bringing alignment to their relationship. The compromise and negotiation involved in consensual activity mature a relationship — consensual motives supersede divergent ones.

Further details on how to achieve consensus are given in Chapter 8.

The factors that overcome the barriers in relationships and make marriage work have not been invented in a Californian pop psychology think tank. They emerge spontaneously in an ideal marriage, as some of them do in real marriages. The ones that do not can be intentionally brought into a conscious marriage, allowing the intrinsic pattern of a healthy relationship to unfold. Chemistry, common goals, commitment, communication and consensus make a relationship effective — they make marriage work. Each is necessary for a marriage to reach its potential synergy; when all the factors are present, a couple will accomplish so much more than the partners ever could separately.

EXERCISE: EXAMINING THE FIVE CS IN YOUR RELATIONSHIPS

The presence of the Five Cs help a relationship; their absence hurts it. All intimate relationships have the factors of chemistry, common goals, commitment, communication and consensus in varying degrees. Being aware of how your past relationships or your current one rates can be helpful in identifying the causes of problems and how to solve them.

In a particular relationship, each of the Five Cs can be rated on a scale from 'strong' to 'weak': five points for strong, one for weak. Two, three and four are for intermediate strength of each factor, but three won't tell you much. If you think a factor's strength in a relationship rates somewhere between two and three or between three and four, try to use the two or the four. Rating several of your relationships may reveal a trend; for example, perhaps consensus always gets a one, indicating a problem with handling competition. Using this rating technique, you may be able to actually identify the reason your past relationships ended, or why your current one has problems. In the next chapter an expanded version of this exercise may prove even more helpful in assessing your relationship history.

3   MAPPING RELATIONSHIPS

Whoever denies the past runs the risk of repeating it.

Richard von Weizaecker

When Angela and Glen met in the same professional programme at university, they felt as if they always had known each other. They had a romantic courtship, they fell in love, and they decided to spend their lives together. Married shortly after graduation, Angela and Glen opened an office together and settled into a rewarding pattern of work and leisure. It seemed like they shared everything: problems came up, but they always had the time, energy and motivation to solve them together.

A year-and-a-half into their marriage, Angela was pregnant. She continued to work until their first son was born and returned to work shortly thereafter, leaving Derrick in the care of her widowed mother during the day. In another few months she was pregnant again — Glen and Angela had always wanted a large family. Once more Angela worked through the pregnancy, but it was not as easy this time. She was fatigued and minor complications developed. When their daughter was born, Angela elected to stay home for a while after the birth, because she felt she had missed an important part of motherhood the first time around. Glen immersed himself in work to provide for his burgeoning family. Ten weeks after Clarissa was born, Angela realised she needed to stay at home and be a mother for longer than she had imagined; her own mother was aging, and caring for two babies would have been too much to ask.

Glen started seeming distant to his wife at about this time. Problems, it seemed, were now left hanging rather than being resolved. Angela now felt like she was watching Glen perform a circus act juggling all the things in his life — her included — while riding a bicycle on a tight-rope. What was worse, Glen felt that that was exactly what he was doing. Two years later Angela was humiliated to find the evidence that Glen was having an extramarital affair.

When Angela confronted Glen, as she knew she must if she was to retain her self-respect, it at first made things between them worse than ever. Angela hung on for several months and finally felt vindicated when Glen asked for her forgiveness. They decided to have another child to seal their reconciliation — it only sealed their fate. After Darren was born Angela vowed she would return to work as soon as she could. They would get back to the way things had been. But it would take years now, instead of months, and by the time three more had passed, it was all over for Angela and Glen.

When the divorce was final, Glen married his girlfriend. Eighteen months later Angela remarried a 'wonderful' man who loved and adopted the three children. The irony of it was that Glen once more took his sex life outside of his new marriage and Angela found to her sorrow, some years and two more children later, that she had married another man who was doing the same. Glen's and Angela's second marriages ended in divorce too.

Most of us would respond to the question, 'How many versions of this case have you seen?' with an answer along the lines of 'Too many'. In another situation, Glen's lack of commitment could have been substituted with excessive drinking, emotional or physical abuse, or other signs of chaos in an unhappy combination.

Like Angela and Glen, too many women and men have cycled through relationships as if they were on automatic pilot. The experience can feel like being caught in a machine, thrashed about and spat out the other end. Most of us are hard pressed to understand what has happened, being preoccupied with picking ourselves up, nursing wounds and getting out of the machine's path for fear it will make a return pass. *It is natural to want a workable intimate relationship, but it can be devastating to be the victim of repeated failure in its pursuit.* Yet despite sincere resolutions to the contrary, so many well-intentioned people are compulsively drawn back into relationships only to be shocked awake as they fly out of the machine's exit time and again. It is the unconscious and compulsive nature of this pattern that is disturbing. In fact, it can be so disturbing that some people repeatedly deny it has ever happened. . . even though it continues to happen to them! Two or three marriages and children later the tell-tale signs are not so easily ignored.

MAPPING RELATIONSHIP: AVOIDING THE HAZARDS

No one can grasp the infinite complexity of life, human beings and their relationships. Whether it be five million army ants behaving as one entity in a Brazilian rainforest, the intricate workings of the billions of neurons in the human brain, the trillions of combinations possible in the human genetic makeup or the zillions of things that can apparently go wrong in a marriage — everyone is equally baffled. Yet, scientists study and learn from the activities of the army ant colony and the brain, and are in the process of mapping the genetic makeup of human beings. Why can't we learn from the successes and failures of our relationships?

In this chapter we will continue to draw a map of effective relationship by adding on to the Five Cs. This is a map of the development of an effective relationship, not a map of all relationships, of the only type that works, or how a relationship should be. Conscious marriage is a model which uses this map that couples may wish to follow in designing their own marriage. There are many ways to go; every couple must find their own way. The map sketched in this book recommends a pragmatic approach. It has been drawn in an attempt to give couples the greatest possible chance of success.

No matter how accurate a map may be, it will never encompass the complexity of the natural world, but a good one will enable you to get from point A to point B. On a whitewater rafter's map, the dangers will be clearly marked: the rocks, the rapids and the odd waterfall, as well as the rest areas and campgrounds. Likewise, a relationship's course has its obstacles and positive features. No one wants to fall victim to life's complexity and unexpected periodic chaos. *By understanding what can go wrong in relationship — or what has gone wrong in your past relationships — you can avoid its hazards.*

THE STAGES OF EFFECTIVE RELATIONSHIP

On their journey together, couples in a growing relationship pass through stages — meeting, courtship, living together, marriage and mature marriage or family. The Five Cs of an effective relationship — chemistry, common goals, commitment, communication, consensus — have a corresponding place in these stages. After their first meeting, or even after knowing one another much longer, if their *chemistry* is right a couple will decide to see one another to further the contact between them. At this point the couple begin a *courtship*, although today they would rarely label it as such. If it is successful, they start planning a future together based on their common goals. It will be apparent, perhaps to others before to the couple themselves, if they are 'having a relationship'. These days having a relationship leads to *living together*. Some degree of commitment allows this to happen. A couple who stay together will either decide to get married or find themselves legally married de facto if they do not part. The relationship becomes a *marriage*. Communication then becomes crucial for the marriage to work. A married couple enter the fifth stage of relationship, *mature marriage or family*, and this usually occurs with the birth of their first child. Continued effectiveness means consensus here.

Of course, nothing in life progresses in such a strict linear fashion — the nature of the model I am presenting here is also cyclical. However, for the purposes of gaining a basic understanding of the elements involved in relationship, we need to first examine the model in its most basic form.

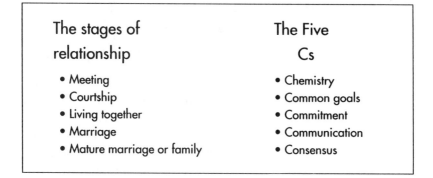

The stages of relationship	The Five Cs
• Meeting	• Chemistry
• Courtship	• Common goals
• Living together	• Commitment
• Marriage	• Communication
• Mature marriage or family	• Consensus

DEVELOPMENTAL STAGES: TASKS AND CRISES

Even though they may not be aware of it, at each particular stage a couple are working on something. This feature of a couple's development parallels an aspect of individual growth well known to psychologists: the developmental task. A developmental task is what ideally happens between a couple at a particular stage. Specific developmental tasks occur at each stage of a relationship, when the presence of the appropriate one of the Five Cs is paramount to the continued development of the relationship. In other words, a developmental task involves the challenge a couple need to rise to if their relationship is to continue successfully. Difficulty with achieving this causes a developmental crisis in the relationship. This is when the relationship hits a barrier and teeters back and forth on the knife-edge of competing forces. At the turning point of each stage, the relationship will move forward if, and only if, one of the Five Cs comes in on its own or is consciously added by the couple.

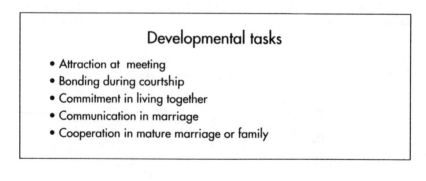

Developmental tasks

- Attraction at meeting
- Bonding during courtship
- Commitment in living together
- Communication in marriage
- Cooperation in mature marriage or family

During their courtship, for example, a couple don't think of getting to know each other as an intentional activity: 'We are going to bond together'. Getting attached to one another just starts happening. At some point, they may begin to wonder if the relationship will work or not, if they are really choosing the right partner, if they want to get so close to that someone. Doubts can escalate to anxiety and even to panic. One partner or both may question whether their involvement is really going anywhere. They may get quite distraught about it. This is a developmental crisis in their relationship. If they are lucky or wise, at the bonding crisis a couple will take stock of their compatibility, of all they have in common — all the plans they have been considering, all the common goals they share in life — and the crisis will advantageously resolve.

As stated, each stage has its own task or developmental theme, its own crisis, and its own crucial factor: one of the Five Cs. Although in the first stage a couple can't do much about it, the task is attraction. The crisis is one of inclusion, and, as we know, chemistry is the factor that resolves it. The second stage has bonding as its developmental task, which leads to a crisis of compatibility. Common goals in a relationship allow a couple to pass through the crisis. In the third stage, trying to develop a commitment brings a couple to a crisis which is resolved positively by making a commitment to each other. The fourth stage, marriage, brings the task of developing effective communication. A couple may have been talking to each other perhaps for months or years, but after making a commitment the communication between them becomes crucial. The outcome of the communication crisis is function or dysfunction. Effective communication resolves it. In the fifth stage of their relationship, mature marriage or family, a couple take on the task of cooperation, face the crisis of power struggle, and can pass through it with consensus.

Sadly the world is full of people who keep getting to a particular stage in relationship and then fail to go on. Typically the relationship ends, and the cycle is restarted with another partner, taken to the same point, where the same crisis is not favourably resolved because the same barrier is not confronted and overcome. Angela and Glen, along with many others, have been caught in this revolving door. For them, it hinged on a lack of commitment. Similar cases routinely produce results spanning the spectrum from

The map of an effective relationship

Stage	Theme	Crisis	What makes it work
Meeting	Attraction	Inclusion vs exclusion	Chemistry
Courtship	Bonding	Compatibility vs directionlessness	Common goals
Living together	Commitment	Exclusivity vs uncommittedness	Commitment
Marriage	Communication	Function vs dysfunction	Effective communication
Family	Cooperation	Cooperation vs power struggle	Consensus

comic to tragic, and create family situations in which five children from three previous marriages are expected to be one big happy family.

Developmental tasks and crises can be overwhelming at first exposure: Nonetheless, understanding the dynamic process of a relationship's development can help a couple to negotiate the difficult times successfully. Recognising that challenges can be brought on by the natural cycle of things — and are not always due to personal inadequacies or a couple's incompatibility — can help you to be more objective in dealing with them: it can help you to see the challenges as positive learning experiences rather than as tests to pass or fail. To clarify the model further for you, I will go through the map of relationship stage by stage.

A MAP OF EFFECTIVE RELATIONSHIP

Meeting

Meeting, the first stage of relationship, begins in various ways. Whatever the circumstances of their first meeting, without the development of attraction, the acquaintances may become friends, the friends may become co-workers, but they won't start to fall in love. If the attraction is strong enough, a relationship, although a new and fragile one, will start. Though the couple may scarcely have noticed, the crisis of inclusion vs exclusion resolved positively — they included each other in a life together. Because they had chemistry, they were attracted to each other. They will meet again to further their contact.

Courtship

In this second stage of a relationship's development, a couple who have been attracted to each other and may be falling in love, enter into a period of intentional contact to the end of more thoroughly checking one another out. The developmental theme of bonding dominates their contact. For bonding to occur a couple must be compatible.

The linear and cyclical nature of the map

It is difficult for some people to understand that the developmental model is *both* linear and cyclical. However, if you can it will be much more useful to you.

The map is linear in the sense that the stages come one after the other. You can tell where a couple are at by identifying the particular stages that have been reached, or not; a couple either do live together or they do not, for example.

No matter what particular stage couples have reached, they tend to cycle through the developmental tasks from all of the stages. A couple might even cycle through the developmental tasks of all the stages in one afternoon: they get together, the chemistry is right, they are attracted and make love. The couple are so compatible in bed that they reach a level of intimacy neither had ever experienced, a goal of both of theirs, and form a kind of bond as a result. This triggers thoughts about commitment for both. Unfortunately that evening they might get into an argument about where to go for dinner, which turns into such a power struggle that they don't want to see one another for another two weeks. Later perhaps they will go on to deeper levels of the developmental tasks they are having trouble with — communication and cooperation — as they continue the cyclical process.

Back on the linear side they have met, they have been attracted and have even begun to bond. At some point they may reach the living together stage, but, of course, they may then argue about who will cook dinner.

The section 'A map of effective relationship' looks at couples' development from the linear perspective, while the section after that 'Relationship growth and developmental model' stresses the cyclical nature of the process.

There are two schools of thought about what constitutes compatibility. One stresses similarity in personality as the determining element; the other stresses complementarity or fit. Sometimes a mixture of both is involved; for example, a doer and a thinker may complement one another, and both be shy. Whether the partners begin to develop enough affinity to contemplate a serious relationship is largely due to how compatible they are. Perhaps you have been attracted to someone you did not 'like'; the explanation may well be that the chemistry was not backed up by compatibility.

The natural interest of the couple at this stage gravitates towards a mutual evaluation. This takes time, and a couple typically want to spend a lot of time together during their courtship. The other may look good and feel good to be around, but what is he or she really like? Each does his or her best to appear in a favourable light, but whether they bond or not is based on compatibility and shared goals.

The factor of common interests and goals stretches from the mundane to the deeper aspects of life. Do they both like fried eggs, tomatoes and chips for breakfast, or porridge? Are they both drinkers, or does one abstain? Do they prefer an active social life, or do they prefer to stay home with a book? Do they both want to settle down and have children or not? Is politics or religion a problem? All the myriad tastes and idiosyncrasies of interest and areas of involvement that can affect life together are surveyed in the screening process as the couple work toward forging a bond.

Ultimately, for a couple to move into the future together, their separate paths in life must share similarity in destination. If strong enough common goals exist, their paths will come together to form one: they will bond. If interest in the prospect of sharing a life together is supported by the reality of common purpose guiding and bonding them, the couple will begin to confront the issue of commitment.

Living together

Genuine compatibility, if no external barrier blocks their progress, leads to a couple thinking about 'getting serious'. Getting serious in practice means making a commitment, the principle theme of the third stage of a developing relationship. Practically, a couple is faced with the decision to live together or not; the stage takes its name from this fact.

At some point, a couple who have been seeing each other regularly with clear romantic intent will probably begin to wonder if they should live together. This is the normal next step to take in the post-sexual-revolution Western world. If it is not taken, the relationship will probably not progress towards commitment. Another romantic interest could intrude and win one partner's loyalty, or perhaps the frequency of contact will fade as it is clear to the couple that the relationship will not get serious. Living together becomes the ground on which the first battle of commitment is fought. The prospect of sharing residence intensifies the couple's focus on their relationship. Living together, or perhaps just discussing the possibility, will often precipitate the crisis of exclusivity vs uncommittedness. Although exclusive commitment in the sexual sense may have already been a criterion for the relationship, each partner now faces the choice to make that commitment long term. Such a decision involves recognising the special value of the other person in one's life and the preparedness to act upon that to strengthen and protect the relationship so that it can develop further. A real degree of sacrifice is necessary for exclusivity to be incorporated into a relationship and a commitment to one another to be made — but the opportunity for further growth and the potential depth of intimacy afforded to the couple is well worth it.

If they choose to live together, it is an importnt landmark in the relationship. The commitment stage may also involve becoming engaged to be married. That will often be demonstrated to the community by the display of some observable sign, a ring or other piece of jewellery for example.

Marriage

When commitment leads to marriage, the fourth stage, the crucial question then becomes: will the marriage work? A couple's ability to communicate answers the question. The developmental task of this stage is improving the relationship through communication.

Having lived together for some minutes, hours, days, weeks, months or, in some cases, years, a married couple will enter a bona fide crisis. The question of how marriage works stops being theoretical and becomes immediate. 'How can *my* marriage with *him* or *her* possibly work?' Encountering this shock occurs when a couple begin to hit the limits of their ability to communicate. Many marriages do not ever work because of bad communication. In days gone by men often got 'cold feet' at this stage (and sometimes used them), while women 'went home to mother'. Virtually every couple who attempt to have authentic, honest and open communication will run into this crisis. The way through the crisis is for the couple to increase their combined ability to communicate. Effective communication develops if a couple are able and willing to persevere in relating to one another. The nuts and bolts of effective communication are given in Chapter 7.

Mature marriage or family

In the fifth stage, the mature or family stage, the main task is the development of cooperation. Consensus is the factor which will promote cooperation between a couple. In consensus, a couple accept one another's power of choice in making the joint decisions taken in the marriage. The conflict between the partners' desires to have their own way and their willingness to accept consensus as an operational principle in the relationship precipitates a crisis. If this crisis is not resolved in favour of cooperation, the relationship may well degenerate into a power struggle which will cripple the marriage. The relationship may even regress into dysfunctional communication, shaking the commitment between the couple. An ugly power struggle can reverse the growth in a marriage and destroy it — while the development of cooperation will sustain it to maturity.

A marriage may mature without becoming a family; competition can be resolved within the relationship through cooperation. However, couples are often plunged into the crisis of cooperation by the birth of a child; hence the other name of the fifth stage, family. A child is often a maturing influence in a relationship as its needs are accommodated by husband and wife who must become less self-centred to cooperate as a family. Power sharing must become the norm.

RELATIONSHIP GROWTH AND THE DEVELOPMENTAL MODEL

A map is not the countryside. As with all models, this developmental model of marriage is only a representation of reality. It would be best considered to demonstrate how an ideal couple might behave in relationship: at each stage the developmental task would be thoroughly completed and the crisis completely resolved. Almost all *real* couples will only partially complete the successive developmental tasks, and consequently will from time to time exhibit symptoms of the problems that brought them to their original crises. During the history of their relationship, all couples — even those who are growing — will at times show varying degrees of incompatibility, feel less than fully committed, communicate poorly, and show signs of competitiveness and power struggle. This is normal. These are the growing pains of relationship.

Couples often take two steps forwards and one step backwards. They may at times doubt whether they are growing. If a couple sincerely wish to have an effective relationship, they will routinely confront problems that arise. They recognise that the ability to deal effectively with problems teaches them more about themselves, each other and the relationship. Persistence with personal growth will ensure that crises eventually give way to renewed attraction, a strengthened bond, deepened commitment, enhanced ability to communicate and increased cooperation.

Couples will cycle through the stages of relationship, happily skipping through developmental tasks they are better at, and dwelling on those that are harder for them. All couples will be stronger in some areas and weaker in others; different barriers will be harder or easier for different couples to break down. If, on balance, a couple's relationship is viable, the developmental tasks will recur as weak areas re-emerge to be strengthened by renewed growth. (Some couples who are especially weak on one particular factor will exhibit characteristic symptoms, described in Chapter 9, because the overall development of their relationship has been impaired by the deficit.) Couples who continue to grow will repeat the developmental tasks until all of them have been satisfactorily completed. Each task has several levels, so a couple more accomplished in tasks in the earlier stages may find themselves, for example, locked in competition early on. This happens because this is the task that needs attention by them. Another couple may be very cooperative but struggle with communication from the first. At any stage, the influence of the factors that make marriage work may be brought to bear consciously by a couple to facilitate growth. In the next five chapters we will explore strategies to maximise the influence of the Five Cs.

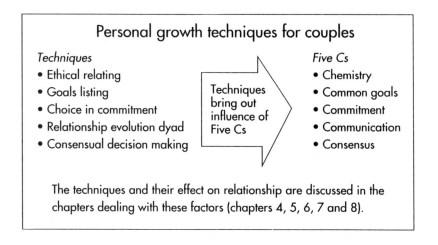

Personal growth techniques for couples

Techniques
- Ethical relating
- Goals listing
- Choice in commitment
- Relationship evolution dyad
- Consensual decision making

Techniques bring out influence of Five Cs

Five Cs
- Chemistry
- Common goals
- Commitment
- Communication
- Consensus

The techniques and their effect on relationship are discussed in the chapters dealing with these factors (chapters 4, 5, 6, 7 and 8).

There is a difference between relationships that are growing in spite of their problems and ones that are destroyed by them.

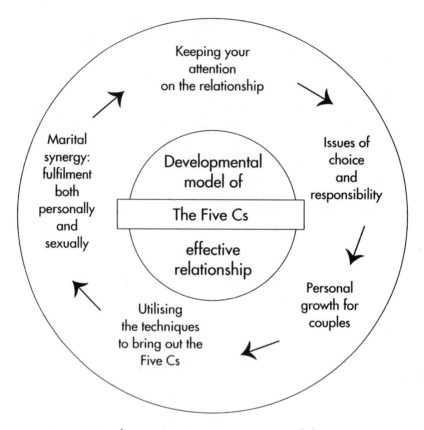

The conscious marriage model

The inner circle of the diagram indicates that the stages of the developmental model (meeting, courtship, living together, marriage, mature marriage or family) are central to the growth of an effective relationship. They are the physical stages couples pass through as tasks and crises either draw them together or push them apart. The outer circle shows the path of personal and relationship growth provided by the conscious marriage model. The central band indicates that the Five Cs (chemistry, common goals, commitment, communication, consensus) are fundamental to both developing relationships and conscious marriages. They bridge both models; occurring spontaneously in the developmental model as the relationship progresses, and with deliberate introduction in the conscious marriage model (with the help of techniques such as ethical relating, goals listing, the exercise of choice in commitment, the discovery that can be found in doing relationship dyads, see page 95, and consensual decision making).

Individuals who have cycled through a series of relationships are the victims of growth being repeatedly short-circuited by the forces pulling their relationships apart. They never make it past a particular barrier. At any stage, the development of a relationship can stop. When the process is interrupted, the developmental task at a particular stage has not been completed because the key factor, one of the Five Cs, has not sufficiently come into play and the crisis has not been advantageously resolved. If a woman and a man who meet lack chemistry, they will not be attracted; if a couple who are assessing one another's suitability for bonding in the courtship stage have too few common goals, their relationship will lack direction and will develop no further; if a couple who are living together cannot make a commitment, their relationship's development will stop; in marriage, a relationship will be dysfunctional if effective communication is not present; in the mature stage, a couple's relationship will devolve into a power struggle if consensus does not become a part of their style of relating. In each case the relationship might not end but, from the viewpoint of effectiveness, it will be ill-fated, unless the couple resume their growth.

EXERCISE: EXAMINING BARRIERS TO YOUR RELATIONSHIPS

Taking a close look at your relationship history in light of the model of the stages and crises of relationship will offer you the opportunity to isolate how and where the process is typically interrupted for you, and provide you with clues for solving recurrent problems. This way of looking at your relationship history, by rating the strength of the Five Cs in your relationships, will deepen your insights. You may even find it helpful to reread the preceding sections, keeping questions like the following in mind: At what stage have my previous relationships run into trouble? What was my awareness of the difficulty at the time? Is that what the problem really was? What could I have done differently? What is it about me that contributed to the relationship's difficulties? What are the strengths and weaknesses of my current relationship in light of my relationship history? What areas of concern should I have about a future relationship, or my current relationship's future?

Nearly everyone's relationships are influenced by the patterns they were exposed to in their family of origin. By using the above technique to assess the strengths and weaknesses of your parents' marriage, you can gain valuable insight into your own possible strengths and weaknesses in relationship.

4

CHEMISTRY, LOVE AND ETHICS

When people begin to take responsibility for their own moral decisions on their own shoulders, they begin to be moral. Theology masquerading as divinely revealed religion has forbidden them that right long enough, and it has thereby produced, quite without anybody intending it, a monstrous amount of ethical impotence, stupid conduct, cruelty, fear and asinine blundering on the part of human beings who would have done well enough if they had been taught to follow that inner craving for what is just, right and beautiful which is the common heritage of all of us.

Lindsay

It is one of the most rewarding things in life, but it is no accident that it is called *falling* in love. The expression — instructively — strains confidence.

'Falling in love' has the connotation of one being helplessly at the effect of unknown forces, presumably natural, but in any event likely to be irresistible. 'To fall' has a few other suspicious meanings: to be severely wounded or killed in battle; to lose one's chastity; to lose power; to be defeated; to yield to temptation; to err or sin; and so forth. It comes as no great surprise that the expression 'falling in love' has caught on. No matter how many songs and poems rhapsodise the experience, no matter how many works of art have been inspired by it, no matter how wonderful it may feel at times, an inescapable fact remains: falling in love often means big trouble. But nature can be tricky. In the first stage of relationship we are led to expect everything, and anything but trouble.

CHEMISTRY, ATTRACTION AND FALLING IN LOVE

When you first meet someone, you can be open to having a relationship with them, but you cannot make a relationship happen wilfully. Some try to convince themselves that they should have or are having a relationship and try to force its development by going through the motions. Almost always they will regret it later. Two people choosing to relate have to 'let it happen'.

Chemistry leads the way to attraction and falling in love. When it is present, chemistry is difficult to deny. Instinctive, emotional and mental components blend to produce it. Structured into each woman's and man's genetic, emotional and mental makeup is a template of attraction. When the sensory impression of someone you know or meet matches your template, a computer-like system flashes alert and the psychophysiology of attraction activates. Perhaps it is realised at first glance, or after years you see that someone has a kind heart and yours melts.

In addition to physical arousal, mental and emotional changes accompany chemistry. An aura of perfection seems to surround the attractive individual: it is as if he or she can do no wrong. To some extent this happens because the brain of the person who has been attracted is being biochemically altered during this time. Feelings of affection and adoration are also produced by chemistry as someone falls in love.

To say a couple are developing a conscious marriage at this point is stretching the model. A couple may be aware they are in love or are on the way, but they don't really have to do much to improve their relationship. For the first eight to twelve weeks — when chemistry is at full tilt — matters move along on their own. Two individuals under the influence of chemistry with its strong psychophysiological effect find it easy to treat one another lovingly. However, make no mistake, the downside of love is real. For a relationship to endure and grow, the regard and affection have to be actively sustained. Understanding the nature of love is the starting point.

To have sex or not to have sex?

Certainly the body will be saying 'Go for it' if chemistry is present: the need to love and be loved will be activated; romantic ideals will fill the mind; social judgments will no longer stand in the way. Yet it may be in your own best interests, and those of the relationship, to wait a while before having sexual contact with a partner at the beginning of a relationship. This is because the forces destructive to relationship will be stimulated by sexual expression. These forces are basically psychological and genetic shortcomings we all have — sex releases energy which activates them. For example, some men become aggresive when they are aroused; or someone may fear abandonment which is triggered by sexual contentment. What you need to do now is to allow trust and love to grow, protect your feelings, and get on with finding out if you and your partner can form a bond, and even a commitment sometime. If you can manage to stay centred — and it is not easy — in the first stage of a relationship, let the sexual energy be there but delay acting on it until it's 'safe', you may be better off in the long run. Sometimes good things come to those who wait.

WHAT IS LOVE?: EROS, PHILOS, AGAPE

Falling in love operates on several levels simultaneously. The intensity of this multilevel experience tends to be all the more overwhelming, confusing and enrapturing as a consequence. More than two thousand years ago, the Greek lexicon had already provided the terminology for understanding what needs to be known about love to support the development of relationship.

Eros

Eros means love and desire: sexual desire, a power so great that it keeps the species going despite quite creative attempts to the

47

contrary. The reproductive instinct is at the root of eros; sexual attraction stems from it. Eros grounds the attractive forces which draw couples together. A familiar intensity surrounds eros, bringing pleasure and pain to couples. The culmination of sexual desire in orgasm strikes like a lightning bolt into a relationship, changing it forever. Eros' irresistible quality forces couples to come to terms with their sex life or face the possibility of compulsion, frustration, conflict or even betrayal.

Philos

Philos is dear love, the love of friendship and family. Philos pulls lovers together at the heart, whereas eros pulls them together at the genitals. Philos underlies the social bond in love. Falling in love means finding a real friend as well as a lover. Philos answers a deep longing in an individual to be together with another, one who cares, understands, and shares life's joys and sufferings. Philos brings loyalty, devotion and willingness to sacrifice to a relationship, moderating eros' intense passion. Philos — human love — nurtures and sustains but has, like eros, a flip-side. Human love can cloy and cling, fostering dependence and the entanglement of co-dependence.

Agape

Falling in love has a spiritual element, as well as physical and emotional ones. This is because of agape. Agape is higher love, divine love. That which is divine recognises the same quality in the other when two individuals fall in love. Agape opens the vistas of love to the infinite and accounts for the uplifting thrill of falling in love. The disadvantages of higher love without the balancing effects of eros and philos are headiness and abstraction between a couple.

In combination

The combination of the spiritual component of love with human love and sexual desire creates a confusing contradiction: how can something so down and dirty, be so friendly and so spiritually uplifting as well? It seems inconsistent, almost sacrilegious, and can be bewildering. Should a couple value or encourage one of the three kinds of love more than the other to any great and long-lasting extent, then the relationship will be unbalanced. The fact is that love *is* instinctive, human and divine. For a marriage to truly work it must embrace this entire reality.

	Forces holding a couple together	Forces pulling a couple apart
Eros (sexual desire)	Sexual attraction: the procreative instinct	Sexual frustration; conflict; compulsive sexuality
Philos (dear love)	Emotional bond: the desire to love and be loved	Dependence; co-dependence; emotional demands and blackmail
Agape (divine love)	Spiritual contact: the desire for a better life in relationship	Abstracted contact; airiness

THE TROUBLE WITH LOVE

Denial and failure to integrate the holistic nature of love is the chief reason why falling in love can lead to trouble. In practice, if agape and philos are denied, eros can run a relationship into the ground. The negative connotations of 'falling' warn against this downside of being struck by Cupid's arrow: to lose power, to be defeated, to err or sin. This is the warning inherent in the expression 'falling in love'. A good example of the potential negative effects of eros' gravitational pull is sex addiction. Some individuals literally become habituated to the biochemicals produced by sexual attraction and contact: biochemicals such as phenylethylamine, the brain's own amphetamine, and the neurotransmitters it releases. Ironically, the frustration of sexual repression is just as undesirable. While sexual desire, unleashed or suppressed, threatens to drag a relationship down, divine love elevates and gives meaning to a relationship, while human love nurtures it, sustains it and holds it together. Without a higher love and friendship a relationship can degenerate and lose its appeal. Frankly, the instincts will lead to having sex, sleeping and eating and then having sex, sleeping and eating — on and on and on. Clearly couples deserve more.

Despite its beneficial qualities, human love can also go awry. Co-dependence is psychology-speak for the underbelly of philos. The unhealthy relationship between an alcoholic and his spouse came to be labelled 'co-dependent' about twenty years ago. The term has become generalised to mean collaboration in addiction. Human love can be as emotionally addictive as heroin or cocaine, and it is much more common. A co-dependent couple *need* each other to be okay. There is no balance between the needs of the individual partners and those of the relationship, because the individuals' needs have all been absorbed by the demands of the relationship. The couple make destructive emotional demands on each other, struggle and manipulate, and can become cut off from social reality. The co-dependent couple have relinquished their power of choice to relate to their love addiction. To some degree all love relationships have a co-dependent element. Therapy is often needed to break addictive patterns — even patterns of emotional addiction. Many of the techniques in this book can help a co-dependent couple and many couples with co-dependent tendencies to recover their ability to choose in relating.

Other couples seem never to come down from the rarefied air of their spiritual connection. In this scenario agape is not balanced by philos and eros. An exclusively mental love can isolate a couple from one another emotionally and sexually, surrounding them with an airy unreality. They need to be grounded by eros and nurtured by philos. Such couples are often lonely, even while they are 'together'. Balance is the key.

There is more to a fulfilling love life than either eros, philos or agape can provide alone. Without the grounding, nurturing *and* uplifting elements of love, a relationship will lack balance and falter — it will fail to grow. If higher love and friendship are integrated with sexuality, the natural course of a conscious marriage will unfold. At some point a couple do not really have to make relationship work — all they have to do is get out of the way and let it work. However, this is a subtle process to regulate; wilful action and surrender alternate. How can a couple practically bring together the different aspects of love? Attending to their relationship will surely help. However, most couples need clear ground rules for their behaviour to one another.

ETHICS IN RELATIONSHIPS

If you want to land on your feet, attend to improving your relationship when you fall in love. A couple can preserve the forces holding them together and guard against the downside of falling in love with ethics in their relationship.

People often feel uncomfortable when the subject of morality comes up — with good reason. Morality prescribes correct behaviour. The problem with morality is that it is often externally imposed, monitored and enforced. That a school, church or state dictate how to act, tends to create as much bad conduct as good behaviour by giving people something to rebel against. This happens even if the behaviour prescribed happens to be right. Enforced morality engenders mistrust and rebellion. External authority overrides individual conscience and choice.

The suppressiveness of traditional marriage led to the rebellion of counter-traditional marriage. Yet too often couples treated each other badly in both. Conscious marriage recommends a higher standard to couples. For the purpose of encouraging a healthy relationship, a couple may choose to hold themselves to an internal ethical system: a set of moral principles they develop themselves. Choosing to adopt ethics that support relationship becomes a pragmatic undertaking if a couple want their relationship to work. If a couple follow ethics when they fall in love, it is much less likely that trouble will result, and the chances of them building an effective relationship are substantially enhanced.

It is highly practical for a couple to apply ethics in their relationship. The philosophy of pragmatism, developed by Charles Pierce (a philosopher) and William James (a philosopher and psychologist) around the turn of the century, is based on the idea that *the value of a course of action lies in its observable consequence.* It is pragmatic for a couple to follow ethics in their relationship because doing so supports the development of an effective relationship. If a couple treat one another well, their relationship will improve. Ethical behaviour results in respect and intimacy between a couple. Ethics hold the forces destructive to a relationship at bay; behaving unethically unleashes them. Destructive forces include abusiveness, the subconscious (our hidden, unacknowledged fears and agendas), lack of commitment, dysfunctional communication and competitiveness. Guilt is one of the worst, and most common, of them all.

Guilt

Guilt causes many relationships to fail, without the couple even being aware of it. If you act badly in your own estimation, you will feel guilty; if you treat your partner badly, it will hurt the relationship. Guilt makes you hold back, withdraw

---

Ethical relating

In a conscious marriage a couple follow ethics in their relationship. They understand that treating each other well brings them closer, and treating each other carelessly creates distance between them. Starting in the first stage of their relationship, they take responsibility for improving it by adopting and following an ethical system.

---

psychologically, create distance between you and your partner. This is self-defeating since development in relationship naturally moves toward intimacy. Guilt also lowers self-esteem. You cannot show respect to your partner if you lose your respect for yourself.

If a couple really do want a workable relationship, adopting and adhering to a set of ethical principles is a logical step in that direction. It is simply a matter of doing what it takes to make the relationship work, and taking responsibility for improving it. Too few couples realise that ethics are a necessary precondition for a relationship's effective development.

To follow moral principles — or not — is a matter of choice for a couple. Only if ethics are freely chosen will their influence be beneficial to a relationship. In considering principles they might wish to adopt, a couple will discover that some moral values are universal and would be included in any ethical system designed to support a relationship's growth.

Non-injury, truthfulness and honesty
Non-injury

If a basically psychologically healthy individual feels at heart that he or she is hurting another physically, emotionally or mentally, he or she will pull back from relating. This backing off in the contact may be subtle. Guilt-based psychological withdrawal often will not even be a conscious decision. It happens because deep down everyone abhors injury; no one really wants to hurt another. Thus non-injury is at the head of the list of universal moral principles. *Injury destroys relationship, non-injury preserves it.*

The dynamic of injury and withdrawal going undetected can cripple or destroy a relationship. Relationship is a sensitive living process that will die if one or both partners stop relating because they feel guilty.

Someone who does want to hurt his or her partner, perhaps by inflicting repeated emotional and physical abuse, is not psychologically healthy. His or her deep desire to love others has become twisted. Emotional pain may be overwhelming their sense of guilt, turning off an important governor of behaviour. Consequently such a person will have a difficult time participating in a constructive relationship. They will probably need more assistance than trying to follow an ethical system can provide. First they must look inside to discover why they are behaving in this way if they are to recover the ability to love and be loved.

Truthfulness

Truthfulness is indispensable to an effective relationship. Telling the truth means verbally stating the facts to the best of your ability. The truth creates reality between a couple while lies create unreality. *Truthfulness is so basic to effective relating that if it is not present the relationship will not stand a chance of working.* A relationship will exist, but it could eventually bear more resemblance to a bad dream than waking reality.

Not telling the truth can disrupt and even destroy an otherwise solid relationship. The white lie is winked at by popular culture, but can turn darker if a couple close their eyes too far too often. Take the case of the working husband who lies about the amount of a bonus to his spouse and uses the money to treat his friends. Harmless white lie? In fact, it is just such instances of verbal duplicity that can come between a couple. The financial resources of a family are a shared resource. Money and sex represent energy in a marriage. When energy is taken away from its proper pathway between the partners the relationship will be affected. Both partners need to know what happens to their money; lying about money makes this impossible. The negative effects of lying to a partner about sex or money can spiral into a pattern of negative behaviours, with guilt, defensiveness and attempts at self-justification on the part of the offender all working to destroy the truth, and thus the relationship. A possible consequence is that the offending husband might become critical of the *wife's* spending behaviour because of his guilt over his own. A fight could start that could damage the relationship. The scary thing about this kind of scenario is that *neither partner may ever really know the underlying dynamic that disturbed their life together.* It is simple: unethical behaviour creates distance between a couple.

Honesty

Honesty is a close relative of telling the truth. Honesty means not hiding the truth. Honesty is synonymous with being forthcoming, telling the other what he or she should know. Failure to be honest may result in a lie of omission. Sometimes people play the mental game with themselves of withholding the truth and then thinking they have not erred because what they *did* say was true. This is rationalising dishonesty. *Dishonesty drains the life energy from relationship.*

In some quarters sexual betrayal is considered to be prestigious. The classic example of dishonesty, epitomising its destructive potential, is failing to tell a spouse about an extramarital affair. The rationale is clear: what someone doesn't know won't hurt them. Wrong! This is an example of the sex and money axiom: there will always be deleterious effects to a relationship if one partner withholds significant data in the sexual realm from the other.

Ethics in conscious marriage

Non-injury: doing no injury
Truthfulness: telling the truth
Honesty: being forthcoming

These three moral principles — non-injury, telling the truth and honesty — constitute a minimal ethical system for a conscious marriage.

If there is injury, lying or dishonesty in any relationship, the attractive force of chemistry will be neutralised or reversed, and a true bond between the individuals will never form, or will be weakened if it has. If unethical behaviour persists or increases, eventually the bond will be broken. Perhaps the couple will stay physically together, perhaps they will never admit to themselves what has happened — let alone why. Perhaps they will pretend they have a good relationship, and go through the motions. The point is, if a couple don't follow these three principles, they will not be able to sustain a functioning relationship. *Without an ethical system it is impossible for a couple to reach the goal of effective relationship.* On the other hand, for a couple who have fallen in love, if unethical behaviour is kept out of their relationship, what remains is the love.

A couple who have a successful relationship are behaving ethically even if they are not aware of doing so. Their values may be so ingrained that they do not consciously think about them. They just naturally treat one another with respect. There are many couples in this category, for whom it seems almost effortless to treat each other with kindness, regard and love. If errors occur, they are corrected as a matter of course. Unhappily, there are far too many couples who do not, cannot or will not do likewise. This may be their choice, or they may be out of control, unaware of what is really going on — that they are actually working to destroy that which may be dearest to them. If a couple want a fulfilling, effective relationship, they must refrain from continually injuring one another. Only then is there a chance for the relationship to grow, to develop, to pass through the stages — to work.

ABUSE CAN STOP A RELATIONSHIP — DEAD

Preferably, *both* partners would adopt an ethical approach to their relationship. There is a potential problem of one partner becoming a victim if he or she tries to follow an ethical code and the other partner does not. The principle that both partners must exercise their choice to improve the relationship for it to grow comes into play. Any two people who cannot agree that non-injury is essential to a relationship leave the door wide open for trouble.

A good opportunity for a couple to discuss the topic of ethical behaviour, and non-injury as a specific tenet of an ethical system, is the first time real injury occurs between them. This would probably be an emotional injury, but it might be physical. The couple should take the opportunity to affirm that they will try not to hurt one another in the future. If they cannot agree to take this approach, it should be considered a dangerous signal. If they do agree to try to practise non-injury, and harm repeatedly occurs or escalates, it should be considered an even more serious warning.

Conscious marriage is an approach designed for basically psychologically healthy individuals, so how to handle serious psychological problems is not explored in this book. However, the media is full of examples of domestic violence; as the issue of violence in relationship is a matter of safety (to women especially) and the wellbeing of society, it has been included. This is a sensitive and very serious issue for couples.

A woman who finds herself in a situation of repeated abuse would be well advised to seriously consider ending the relationship. The sooner an intractable abusive relationship is ended, the easier it will be on both parties. Everyone deserves a second chance, as does every loving relationship — but the line must be drawn at unremitting abuse. This does not happen in a loving relationship. Someone may say they love the other, but if they cannot show that

---

If you are in an abusive relationship

What do you do if you are in relationship with a partner who is hurting you? The short answer is, have a safety plan; find someone you can rely on in an emergency, such as a trusted neighbour, friend, family member or counsellor. Plan where you will go if you need to leave a dangerous situation, and how you can obtain immediate support. Get help for yourself and the relationship (if your partner is willing), and be willing to give up the relationship if he is not.

love in the way they behave, it is not a loving relationship. It is a sign of psychopathology — which may be competing with love, and winning. Such a relationship should be abandoned as early as possible, at least until real change occurs. It will be harder to leave later, because the longer the abusive relationship, the greater the chance of violence erupting. If someone who is being abused finds that she does not want to leave or cannot leave her partner, quite simply, she should get help. Someone in this position may be at the beginning of an abusive cycle that could end in serious injury or even death.

Violence is at the opposite pole to an effective relationship — it is love gone wrong. *A relationship cannot grow beyond the attraction stage to develop a healthy bond in the presence of violence.* The danger even exists of developing an unnatural bond, one that is hard to break. Held together by such a bond, a couple can destroy one another. In such instances, the injury between a couple must be stopped if love is to begin forming a healthy bond. This means a couple need to follow an ethical system, by whatever name. They could call it 'The Rules' if that would be more acceptable. *Rule 1: No hitting, no hurting, no violence.*

LIVING ETHICALLY

Learning to live with ethics in a relationship takes time and willpower. No one can follow an ethical system perfectly. No one is perfect, everyone will make mistakes. To successfully apply ethical principles involves wilful effort, self-inspection and persistence. When you realise you have made an error, admitting it to yourself and to your partner can heal a developing rift. Mistakes are then easier to prevent the next time.

Couples need to know that changing human behaviour is not as simple as resolving to adhere to an ethical code. Being committed to work toward the ideal embodied in an ethical system is the most constructive attitude to take. This in and of itself will help the relationship grow. Effort pays dividends. Sincere effort and progress in following ethical principles increases the chances of success in a relationship. From the moment a couple meet and fall in love, following an ethical system becomes crucial to the future growth of their relationship.

EXERCISE: GUILT CLEARING AND ADOPTING AN ETHICAL SYSTEM

Facing up to guilt from past relationships, or from a current one, can help to relieve its debilitating effects on current or future relationships. Admitting errors can be a healing exercise. Guilt's power is strengthened by hiding things you have done or have failed to do. Owning up to mistakes can undercut guilt's power to interfere with relationship.

Guilt clearing is helpful in improving a relationship; however, preventing future guilt by adopting an ethical code is just as important.

Getting in touch with your internal sense of guilt involves honesty in self-inspection. If you wish to reduce the level of guilt in your relationship life, you can start by contemplating what you think you have done in past relationships that you should not have, and what you have failed to do that you think you should have. Mentally approaching it from both sides keeps the process of self-inspection flowing. It may help to write the results down. Five minutes will not be enough to do justice to this procedure. If you have an understanding friend or minister, you may wish to share the results of your self-inspection with them.

Ironically, accurately identifying sources of guilt can help you create and reinforce your own set of moral principles. For example, noticing your guilty feelings about having hurt others (physically, emotionally or mentally), will help support you with trying not to do so in the future. Looking back over your past guilt-causing behaviour is a helpful way to connect to a personal moral system. Originating a system that has personal meaning is more useful than relying on someone else's idea of right and wrong. However, it is always wise to check your self-generated ideas with universal moral principles to fill in blind spots.

For a couple to successfully follow an ethical system, both partners need to responsibly apply their own internal sense of what is right and wrong in light of the moral principles that they have adopted. It is crucial for the success of this approach that both partners are motivated to avail themselves of the benefits of ethics in relationship. If they are not, an ethical system will probably not be followed, and its practical effects will not be felt in the relationship. If you would like to attract a partner willing to apply ethics to relationship, or you want to inspire a current partner to do so, you can begin following an ethical system yourself. Discussing ethical principles with your partner will help to clarify to them the type of behaviour you intend to show them, as well as the type of consideration you expect them to show you. Finding out your partner's thoughts and asking questions to truly understand where your partner is coming from — and being open and honest yourself — are all positive steps to creating a healthy relationship.

5 COMMON GOALS

We do not have to visit a mad house to find disordered minds;

our planet is the mental institution of the universe.

Johann Wolfgang von Goethe

If the subconscious is the great saboteur of relationship, competing goals at cross-purposes between partners are the dynamite. Locked away below the surface of consciousness, competing goals can make a relationship crazy. This dynamic often underlies the conflicts that send plates of spaghetti flying, cause verbal arguments or withdrawn sullen silences. For example, consider the conflict when she has the subconscious goal to be always loved, and he has the subconscious goal to be always independent. Her efforts to receive affection are threatening to him because they appear to challenge his own efforts to be independent, which are threatening to her because they seem like rejection.

In a way, such a conflict supports personal growth by confronting the partners with their psychological issues. How emotionally charged the competing goals are will affect whether the relationship will be workable or not. Often these conflicts can be worked out between partners; sometimes outside help is needed. Some practical self-help techniques are offered at the end of this chapter, which may help you to prevent or minimise such conflicts by making you clearly aware of your own goals and those of your partner.

HANDLING THE SUBCONSCIOUS

The subconscious mind is of dubious reality to many people, but nevertheless, everyone is affected by the hidden desires contained within it. If you have ever responded unintentionally to an apparently innocent comment by a friend or relative with a much more heated response than would seem appropriate, you have experienced an everyday sign of the subconscious at work. Perhaps — embarrassingly — anger or sadness came pouring out.

Carl Jung has described the shadow as that dark, primitive part of the mind that is cast or projected onto the surrounding world, including others. The subconscious colours our perceptions of the world in this fashion. For example, perhaps a person is deeply insecure, but does not know it. Jung would predict that the person would consequently experience the world as a threatening place. To some extent the world *is* a threatening place, but a subconsciously insecure individual would experience it to be particularly so, perhaps indiscriminately so, unrealistically so. The person might even develop paranoid symptoms and see danger around every corner. As the old saw correctly observes: 'Just because you are paranoid doesn't mean they are not out to get you'. However, someone who is not paranoid probably knows the difference between a friend and an enemy. To the paranoid person, everyone presents a potential danger. The point is that, to some degree, everyone's subconscious inner world is projected onto the world outside. Relationship partners often become victims of one another's subconscious minds in this way.

Jung encouraged his patients to analyse their perceptions of the world around them to glean clues to their own inner world. Freud developed the techniques of free association and dream analysis to uncover subconscious material. Making the subconscious conscious is the general principle. It is therapeutic to bring hidden influences into awareness — with awareness you can work to minimise their effects. It would be impractical to subject everyone who wanted to get married to ten years of psychoanalysis. Who knows, even then a couple might still throw plates of spaghetti at each other — but with full knowledge of *why* they were doing it! Fortunately a simple, effective technique, 'goals listing', can help bring our subconscious desires into our conscious mind, and help us translate them into a constructive direction in our relationships. (The

62

technique of goals listing is explored at the end of this chapter.)

It may be a disturbing thought that not only do goals exist below the level of consciousness — they are also pursued. People routinely try to fulfil wishes of which they are not even aware. How satisfying would it be, even if a goal was reached, if you were not aware of having it in the first place or that you were actually pursuing it? Bringing goals into consciousness alleviates this problem.

Becoming aware of goals is even more important for another reason. Some goals are unrealistic or impossible to achieve. Wanting to be always loved or independent are examples of goals that can never be reached. These are neurotic goals. If trying to do something that cannot be done is a definition of neurotic behaviour, something that cannot be achieved is a neurotic goal. The previous example of the conflict between a couple motivated by competing subconscious goals demonstrates this situation. No one can realistically be always loved or always independent. To try to be is a little crazy. Moving your subconscious goals into your consciousness can be therapeutic because you can then subject them to the light of rational judgment; a goal may then be reality tested. The pursuit of neurotic goals is not only futile, it is a set-up for frustration and unhappiness, especially in relationship. When we become aware of and rule out neurotic goals, realistic, achievable goals are left to be pursued. As a result, our chances for happiness are increased, and frustration decreased, in life and relationships.

COMMON GOALS: DIRECTION FOR A RELATIONSHIP

Many people in the world today lack direction. They may behave in a variety of ways, but show no coherent pattern, no evident purpose, to their behaviour. Such individuals do have wishes and motivations — they are just not aware of them. Their desires are locked away in their subconscious mind. This state of affairs can lead to a life of dissatisfaction, drained of meaning.

What do you want out of life?

To be truly satisfied in life you must follow a truer course than others' expectations will ever provide. Knowing what *you* want — from within — is necessary. Then when you make conscious efforts toward reaching your goals — and make progress — life is rewarding. Reaching goals makes you happy! Goals give life direction and meaning.

In a conscious marriage the partners know how important goals are — both individual goals and common goals. Between two people who have fallen in love, a personality fit is not really enough to lead to a meaningful relationship. When the initial excitement fades, problems will develop; for example, the couple may begin to wonder why they are together. If common goals are present, they will provide the answer. *Common goals add a dimension of meaning, forge a bond that will hold it together, and offer direction to a compatible, loving relationship.* Common goals are an important and often neglected factor in making marriage work. They develop compatibility into a bond and prepare a couple for commitment.

Bonding is central to the viability of a relationship over time. Two individuals who are attracted to one another will only be held together if a bond forms. In the second stage of the development of a relationship, the process of bonding occurs if the crisis of compatibility is resolved by finding common goals. Bonding may be thought of as having two phases. For two pieces of a puzzle to stay together, they must first fit together. But even if they fit, they can be pulled apart. Relationship partners must fit together to stay together; this is based on their compatibility. For them to continue to stay with one another, they must bond or they may be shaken apart by the forces destructive to relationship, such as abusiveness, the subconscious mind, etc. Common goals may be thought of as the adhesive that cements the bond in a couple. Although common goals are not enough to ensure that a relationship will reach its natural maturity, without them its future will be dimmer. As a relationship grows and deepens, so too should a couple's shared goals.

Goals shared by a couple serve as a channel through which the energy of relationship can be constructively directed. A healthy relationship will demonstrate the presence of common goals, even if the couple have never intentionally generated them. The couple nonetheless are guided by those goals and united in seeking their attainment.

Analogous to the individual without direction is the couple without the compass of shared aims. Such a couple will suffer. The goalless, or directionless, couple do not know where they are going; they have not discovered a purpose to be together. Their relationship is aimless. A lack of common goals can contribute to their breaking up, because two people lacking common purpose will be more likely to go their own ways than to form a lasting bond.

MEANING IN MARRIAGE: COMMON GOALS

In modern life, marriage and family have been neglected to some extent by the pursuit of professional goals. Often a couple's shared goals are secondary to their individual goals, and to the demands of employment and career. Individual achievement has stepped in to compete with achievement in relationship. Many marriages have suffered accordingly. This trend has led to aimless relationships, families that do not know what they are doing together, and children who go to school with a house key tucked into their pocket. *In a conscious marriage a couple value relationship and personal achievement. This is an important part of balancing personal needs with those of relationship.* If marriage as an institution is to begin working again in Western culture, a re-prioritisation of values, elevating the importance of relationship, must occur. In the last twenty years it has become fashionable for parents to pursue career first; perhaps in the next twenty years it will be 'in' to reverse, or at least re-balance, these priorities.

Sustaining a marital relationship takes stronger common goals than does an adolescent or young adult romantic relationship. There is nothing wrong with a couple sharing interests in music, dancing, sports and having a good time, but many couples find, to their dismay, that such interests are not enough to hold them together when they face the inevitable adversity marriage brings. When crises of compatibility come and recur in a marriage, they cannot be positively resolved in the absence of shared basic goals. If the relationship is to keep growing, the goals must deepen.

As individuals mature, they are confronted with discovering what is important to them in life. A couple would do well to look at this issue before marriage if they want to increase the chances of their relationship surviving. Couples who clarify their goals and values in life and find that they want a good relationship and to get and stay married, will probably have a better chance of doing just that. Having financial stability, a home and family together are also central common goals that will, in all likelihood, increase the probability of compatibility lasting.

Having children is such a strong common goal, fulfilling a deep biological imperative for many people. It can bring such profound satisfaction that couples who want to make a marriage work would be wise to give the matter serious consideration.

Consciously approaching the project of forging a bond by developing common goals can give a relationship a head start as it begins or a boost as it grows. The perspective of conscious marriage is that life has an intrinsic pattern, a course and a direction. Between a woman and a man life unfolds in attraction, bonding, commitment to one another, working out the problems, and, usually, the collaboration of having and raising a family. If a young couple discount the stages of effective relationship in setting their goals together, they risk missing an opportunity to strengthen the forces holding them together.

EXERCISE: GOALS LISTING

A couple who want to get married or, for that matter, a married couple seeking to deepen and strengthen their bond together, would do well to express their goals to one another. This does not mean to sit down over wine and cheese and proceed to have an argument about whose goals in life are right or more important. It means to let the sharing in relationship deepen to include what the two partners truly want out of life. For a couple to share their goals, first they must be aware of them. Goals listing is a technique designed to help an individual become aware of what he or she wants in life. If you do not know what you want out of life, doing goals listing for yourself first will help solve the problem.

There is often a degree of resistance to listing goals, since the subconscious, a very deep and private part of you, is being explored. There is also commonly a surge of energy when unknown goals are allowed to surface, as the psychic energy that keeps them out of consciousness is released. It can be quite a rush. Goals listing is best approached as a form of meditation. If you would like to try it, arrange time and space in your life to do so. A thorough goals list, anything from one hundred goals to as many as a thousand in some cases, will take several hours to compile, perhaps over a period of a week or two. Goals listing has four steps:

Determining personal goals

Step 1: Make a list of goals you have in life, divided into several sub-lists. Include lists of things you *would* like to do, have and be in life. Also make lists of things you *do not* want to do, have, or be. You may wish to alternate between the opposite lists if you find yourself temporarily stuck. Try to let a flow develop. Be as specific or as general as you are inclined. Just let the process happen; suspend your judgment; keep contemplating: 'What do I really want in life?' Make a list of things you have given up on having, doing or being, as well as a list of things that you want that others would not approve of. Finally make lists of what you want in a relationship, and what you want in a partner. Make the opposite lists for these: what you *don't* want in a relationship, and what you *don't* want in a partner.

Step 2: Go back over all the lists and cross out those things which you do not want to pursue at present, and those things that are unrealistic or impossible.

Step 3: Go over the remaining goals and ask the following question of yourself about each of them: 'If I reached this goal, what would I want then?' If a goal holds up to the question, that is, nothing occurs to you to do or be or have after that goal is attained, leave it on the list. Generate a new list from all of the lists. Then repeat Step 2 and Step 3 on the new list, again crossing out goals you would want something else after, until only a few remain. A handful of basic goals should begin to show up by repeating Steps 2 and 3, goals that underlie the others. These are your goals in life.

Step 4: Make a list of the obstacles that oppose the attainment of your main goals, listing four or five obstacles for each goal. Devise strategies for overcoming these obstacles as you work toward attaining the basic goals you have.

Determining shared goals

Communicating their goals to one another allows a couple to be aware of shared goals — deepening the bond between them. It may be done formally or informally, depending on the preference of the couple. The following guidelines may be helpful:

- Tell your goals to your partner simply, but explain what you mean. Tell them one at a time. Tell your partner what he or she needs to know about a goal to understand it fully.
- As you listen to your partner talk about his or her goals, be receptive, refrain from interrupting, except to ask briefly for clarification, and control the expression of any reactions you have to what you hear, including judgment. Judgment can be subtly conveyed in body language: rolled eyes, a raised eyebrow, or appearing distracted.
- Take turns sharing your goals, alternating talking and listening. Don't let one partner dominate the interchange by talking more than his or her fair share.

- Don't respond directly to your partner's goals, or try to counter them with your own. Discussion may follow. The first step is to allow communication of goals to take place.

- Notice the similarities and differences between your own goals and your partner's. Notice how it feels to discuss your own goals and hear your partner's. Try to open yourself to improving your relationship.

- When both partners are satisfied that they have fully expressed what they have to say about their goals, discussion can begin. It is important that neither partner invalidates what the other has to say, but accepts their right to have their own goals. Details on the art of successful communication are given in Chapter 7, and this may help you with your discussion.

6 COMMITMENT

Those whom the gods would humble, they first make proud.

Suave disdain, icy disdain, and on a bad day perhaps jeering disdain meet the mention of commitment. Granted, commitment is no fun, but both sexes protest too much. The truth is that commitment scares and angers men and women alike. A committed, ineffective relationship *is* scary.

The counter-traditional model of marriage rebelled against the suppressiveness of commitment in traditional marriage. This justified rebellion has led to the popularity of an unjustified anti-committed stance. Consequently, the issue of commitment falls into a void — avoid — for many couples; it just slips by as they go on together, only to surface later as a serious problem. Anti-commitment ignores the pragmatic effects of commitment in an effective relationship, as well as the deleterious effects of a lack of commitment — an ineffective relationship.

COMMITMENT: YESTERDAY, TODAY AND TOMORROW

Historically, a commitment might have been made by the wife's father, for example, and the prospective husband or his father. Marriage was synonymous with wedlock, a term that does not exactly evoke a sense of the couple's free will being involved. People virtually had to get married and they had to stay married. Now, at least in Western society, no one has to get married, let alone stay married. Many people have children without getting married. Serial relationships, with or without the formality of a marriage ceremony, compete with marriage and threaten its viability as an institution. The rise of informal relationships, within the framework of a counter-traditional approach, can be partially understood as a natural swing away from the injustices of enforced marriage. The fact is that individuals have choice in the matter. *Commitment is based on choice.* Some of the problems with de facto relationships or serial relationships are beginning to be experienced by those involved, as well as by society as a whole, and conscious commitment in marriage is emerging as an appealing alternative. While making a commitment is a matter of choice, and one with serious consequences, an effective marriage is impossible without it.

Components of commitment

- Conscious choice to stay together.
- Willingness to do and go through what it takes.
- Sexual exclusivity.
- Responsibility to raise the children together.

Commitment between individuals is another one of the necessary factors, along with chemistry and common goals, that make a marriage work. Chemistry brings a couple together, common goals hold them together and commitment keeps a couple together. If the crisis of commitment is resolved, a relationship becomes a marriage. Since commitment is such a charged issue for couples, many never develop it.

The forces arrayed against commitment are formidable, and include:

- a fear of commitment itself, which can spring from a number of sources, including the fear of putting yourself totally on the line for a relationship that may not work out after all;
- an unwillingness to assume responsibility, for example, for

what you may have to go through to make it work;

- rebelliousness against the traditional model, which could be the result of the fear of being tied down, of losing your freedom to do whatever you want to do, or being locked into something that, from witnessing your own parents' marriage, is really scary stuff; and

- the common predilection of both sexes for more than one sexual partner over time, which can seem to challenge you, or cause insecurity.

Couples and commitment

The couple on the verge of living together bump up against commitment — whether or not they are aware of it. They may simply assume that they *are* committed to each other, whether or not they take the step of living together. One partner may assume that they are both committed without even discussing the issue — and the assumption may be wrong. Either partner or both may be reluctant to broach the topic for fear of being considered mistrustful, of questioning the other's sincerity. Perhaps one or both are secretly jealous, whether justifiably so or not, but are embarrassed to admit it. Or they may hold back concerns or feelings about commitment out of a reluctance to be thought 'old fashioned'.

Even if a couple do verbally agree that they are committed, they may not specify what exactly that means to them. If it is left unspecified, invariably commitment will mean different things to the partners, setting up unarticulated expectations. Five, ten or fifteen years into marriage, a vague commitment may not carry much weight. A very important component of commitment is the limit of the commitment. Presumably outright sexual contact with someone else is out of bounds, but what about flirting or hugging? A couple may feel that it is petty to bring up these details. Yet one or both may well feel very uncomfortable witnessing them.

Discussing the issue of commitment openly and honestly, and being specific about what it means to both partners, is essential if a commitment is to work.

Since commitment demands responsibility, sacrifice and perseverance it can be very intimidating. Yet an uncommitted couple can never make their marriage work. Commitment in a conscious marriage combines several essential elements for a couple: the conscious choice to stay together; the willingness to make the appropriate sacrifices and to go through whatever is necessary — within reason — to preserve the union; sexual exclusivity; and the responsibility of raising their children together. The couple who keep growing will probably find themselves trying to incorporate these features into their commitment.

It is not reasonable to expect a spouse to endure repeated emotional, physical or sexual abuse. The days have passed when a couple was almost forced to stay together out of social, religious, legal or economic pressure. A hundred years ago, women lacked the civil rights to function in society without being legally associated with a man. These external pressures holding marriage together have rightly eased, leaving the responsibility for making — and continuing — a commitment to couples themselves.

THE TWO-PRONGED CATCH IN COMMITMENT

Two individuals who consciously choose to stay together have a commitment. However, the very nature of choice means that change is an option. Anyone who chooses to stay together with a partner can also choose to leave. *A couple must not only choose to be together, they must hold that choice through time for a true commitment to exist.* When a commitment of this nature is made, there is a catch. The catch can be looked at from two viewpoints — as a sacrifice, or as a responsibility. However it is viewed, the relationship faces an acid test.

When a couple make a commitment, they begin to experience things they may not be willing to go through. They encounter barriers when commitment begins to bite. The old stereotypes had the male startling in fright upon meeting his newly-wed wife for the first time with her hair in curlers and face covered with cold-cream; and the female, bored to tears as she contemplates her true love, his backside glued to the sofa watching sports, beer in

73

hand, for hours on end. Of course such inelegant scenarios are always more amusing if they are happening to someone else. However, it is an ordeal for everyone who commits to a relationship when the unexpected consequences of making a commitment begin to surface. The inlaws, jealousy, financial pressures, living together, sexual problems — all the varied start-up difficulties encountered in the transition between 'just a relationship' and a committed one make their debut. There is the inevitable internal 'Oh no!' accompanying these experiences, which can rapidly build up, especially without adequate communication, and threaten to break the back of a commitment.

Then there are the real and imagined sacrifices that come with commitment: keeping a partner informed of your schedule, and coordinating schedules instead of just going your own way; sexual exclusivity; giving up the primacy of the closeness to parents; giving up freedom and spontaneity; and on and on. The danger for a relationship is that rather than accepting sacrifice as the logical consequence of the choice to commit, it will be blamed on the partner. This breeds resentment which, if not handled, can grow into bitterness. Emotional immaturity can appear like an old ghost in a Shakespearian tragedy to exacerbate such reactions. *To make a lasting commitment two individuals must be able to put the needs of the relationship before their own, at least when it counts. This is the real sacrifice commitment requires.*

The most direct way to deal with the necessary sacrifice that commitment brings is to accept that choosing involves responsibility. This does not mean to assume an attitude of being burdened by the cares of life and let all joy go out of relationship as a result. It means to accept sacrifice as the price everyone must pay if they are to receive the benefits of commitment. The two-pronged catch of commitment — responsibility: what must be done and gone through; and sacrifice: what must be given up to maintain it — often drags a relationship down. Understanding that these things are a natural consequence of commitment — that they are not due to some malevolent force that wants to see you suffer but rather involve a personal choice to let go of the old to make way for the new — can raise the probability of commitment enduring the tests it will surely face.

The two-pronged catch

Responsibility: what must be done and gone through.
Sacrifice: what must be given up.

One way to prepare for the responsibility of commitment is to take it slowly and in steps. A couple can start by talking about the possibility of making a commitment and what it would mean, considering the advantages and disadvantages. Over time, they can include the realistic responsibilities and sacrifices of the choice to commit in an on-going dialogue. Next, they could make a trial commitment for a month or even six months. Many relationships go through such a period without naming it, and some form of trial period is likely to occur prior to any serious commitment being made. A couple might try living together, getting engaged, taking the step of jointly choosing not to be involved in other romantic relationships, or some combination of these arrangements. The partners would do well to explicitly express their expectations of one another.

SEXUAL FAITHFULNESS IN COMMITMENT

Sexual exclusivity in marriage is more than a matter of AIDS prevention, although it certainly includes that aspect today. To try to have an effective marriage without sexual faithfulness is like going on a picnic in a mine field. Yet instincts wired into the genetic makeup of both men and women to have more than one sexual partner make such forays sometimes seem compellingly inviting. Some couples have even attempted to institutionalise such instincts — without much success. Look askance at anyone who declares that they have an 'open marriage' and that it works. Check in with that couple in two or three years and see how workable it has really been. Ninety-nine times out of a hundred either the marriage will have ended in divorce or separation, or the partners will still be legally joined but will have retreated into resigned distance. The practical consequences of not being committed suggest that *if couples want to take a pragmatic approach to marriage, sexual exclusivity should be included in their marriage vows.* 'Forsaking all others' equals sexual faithfulness in an effective marriage, not to please the church, but simply to avert potential disaster.

MAKING A COMMITMENT: VOWS AND ADVANTAGES

Traditionally, the commitment in marriage was made by taking vows during a religious ceremony. This formal commitment was made in the presence of witnesses. Presumably, the presence of witnesses prevented the new husband or wife from reneging on their vows following a less than felicitous honeymoon. For too many, the formal wedding vow has degenerated into a formality today. Nonetheless, a couple may choose to invest their vows with personal meaning for their union.

A couple wishing to start their marriage with a real commitment, or a married couple wishing to renew or deepen their vows, may take it upon themselves to discuss the issue of commitment and write their own wedding vows. A couple may wish to acknowledge the multi-level quality of their bond in their pledge to each other. For example, their sexual connection may be acknowledged with a vow of sexual faithfulness; their friendship, with a vow to love each other; and their divine connection, with a vow to do their best to incorporate divine love into their union by truly accepting one another. If the couple wish to follow an ethical code in their relationship, they may choose to pledge to be non-injurious, truthful and honest (or to follow the ethical principles they have chosen) in how they treat each other.

THE COMMITMENT OF RAISING CHILDREN

While it is up to a couple whether they choose to bring children into the world or not, if they do an important feature of their marital commitment involves their responsibility to raising their children together. Consciously accepting this before the fact can help a couple stay together when the going gets rough. *In a committed marriage, a couple are willing to take on the responsibility of raising their children.*

WHAT A COMMITTED RELATIONSHIP CAN ACHIEVE

It may seem naive or idealistic to take such a functional approach to commitment; however, it is actually pragmatic to do so. It is naive to expect a marriage to work without an authentic commitment. Anxious over-emphasis on the downside of commitment can obscure its benefits. The fact is that making a commitment to a relationship opens the door to the advantages of a conscious marriage. Passion can be released in a bounded setting, allowing the potential of unbounded pleasure; love can thrive in an atmosphere of mutual trust; the divine connection can be allowed to deepen, guiding and adding meaning to married life. In the context of an effective relationship, a commitment is a good risk, an investment in the future that can bear dividends for a lifetime.

A couple who contemplate, explore and choose commitment have made an important rite of passage. Frankly, it is a monumental relief. To have been alone, or in uncommitted or otherwise ineffective relationships, to have gone through the genuine soul searching and hair-tearing that the process of becoming committed involves, means something very important to most of us. A part of your life is over, a new part of life has begun.

Love flourishes in the environment of commitment on all levels. The solid security commitment brings provides the foundation for a fulfilling sex life. Within the context of a committed marriage, a couple can let their sexuality blossom to derive the pleasure, trust and intimacy it can bring. If a couple let their sexuality flow only within their marriage, they can relax into that flow and let it build. They can *really* relax. The opportunity for letting go to each other in a secure union is an often unappreciated feature of commitment in marriage. Eros' downside is minimised — compulsion and out-of-control behaviour are less likely to become a problem.

Philos expresses itself in deep friendship and emotional closeness in a committed couple. Commitment allows a couple to deepen their contact, and gives them permission to feel vulnerable or needy. The loneliness of a single life becomes a distant memory in a conscious marriage. To have the need to love and be loved fulfilled allows an individual to mature and leave emotional insecurity behind. Emotional demands and the other dangers of

---

Oh no, commitment!

One of the main disadvantages almost any honest person will consider when facing commitment is loss of freedom, especially sexual freedom. Pragmatically, this disadvantage pulls less weight than the little devil whispering in your ear would have you believe. Engaging in a series of sexual encounters, generally leads to diminishing returns of satisfaction. The amount of pleasure experienced in them will eventually decline as their number increases. At the beginning excitement may rise, but after peaking, in all likelihood, it will fall, along with mental health. Those on a course of serial sex may still pretend to be 'sexually liberated' or justify their behaviour in a number of ways, but guilt will eventually take its toll on them. Such scenarios usually end up resembling imprisonment rather than liberation. There is nothing sadder than a lonely old Don Juan or Juanita.

After a commitment is made, a little devil will still whisper in your ear from time to time, making all sorts of seemingly tantalising recommendations. A word to the wise: ignore him and enjoy a committed marriage.

---

co-dependence can be healed with time in a committed couple. As the need to love and be loved is fulfilled, neurotic strategies to meet it drop away, and the couple partake of a rare commodity in today's world — emotional health and wellbeing.

Love is truly a fragile living thing; commitment offers the solid basis it needs to keep growing and the opportunity to integrate love's three levels. Commitment continues the process ethics began in the couple — it is an ethic in and of itself. A good marriage will produce two best friends who help and support one another interdependently. They can rely on each other to work together for the common good of the marriage. Added to a fulfilling sex life, this bond of love enriches a relationship in a fashion that transcends the practicalities and minutiae of life, and actually approaches the possibility of a divine love. Commitment is at the basis of this potentiality.

COPING WITH THE CONTINUING CRISIS

At times all relationships will have periods of crisis, when staying in the relationship seems intolerable. This is a recurrence of the crisis of commitment. Most often crises of commitment recur because one or both partners are finding it difficult to carry out their responsibilities and make the sacrifices necessary to sustain the relationship, or are encountering unacceptable consequences of being committed to the relationship. When such a crisis does recur, commitment becomes shaky.

However, such crises can be useful, as they often point to an adjustment that needs to be made in the marriage. Talking out the issues, compromising with and responding to each other can often resolve problems, leaving the way open for renewed and strengthened commitment.

Intolerable as such episodes may seem when they are in full sway, they would best be accepted as inevitable. The upset involved in a growth crisis is preferable to the grief and unhappiness that may accrue from the choice to leave a marriage. A broken commitment can be devastating to both individuals'

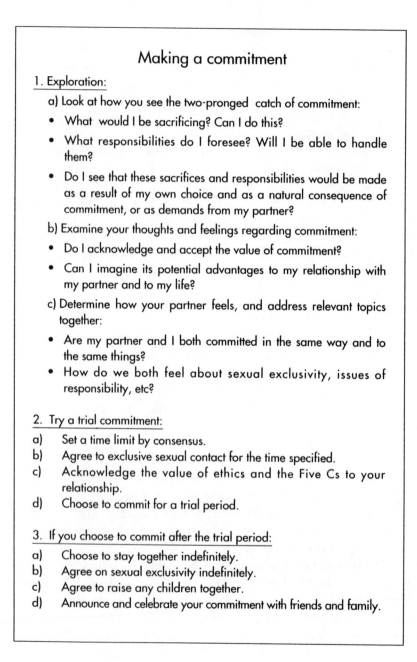

Making a commitment

1. Exploration:

a) Look at how you see the two-pronged catch of commitment:

- What would I be sacrificing? Can I do this?
- What responsibilities do I foresee? Will I be able to handle them?
- Do I see that these sacrifices and responsibilities would be made as a result of my own choice and as a natural consequence of commitment, or as demands from my partner?

b) Examine your thoughts and feelings regarding commitment:

- Do I acknowledge and accept the value of commitment?
- Can I imagine its potential advantages to my relationship with my partner and to my life?

c) Determine how your partner feels, and address relevant topics together:

- Are my partner and I both committed in the same way and to the same things?
- How do we both feel about sexual exclusivity, issues of responsibility, etc?

2. Try a trial commitment:

a) Set a time limit by consensus.
b) Agree to exclusive sexual contact for the time specified.
c) Acknowledge the value of ethics and the Five Cs to your relationship.
d) Choose to commit for a trial period.

3. If you choose to commit after the trial period:

a) Choose to stay together indefinitely.
b) Agree on sexual exclusivity indefinitely.
c) Agree to raise any children together.
d) Announce and celebrate your commitment with friends and family.

future happiness, as well as the wellbeing of children who may be involved. Its consequences should be weighed before irrevocable steps are taken that may be later regretted. As the years pass, a couple in a conscious marriage remember that it is their choice to stay together or not. Choice brought them together, into and through the crisis of commitment, and only choice will keep them together.

EXERCISE: WHAT COMMITMENT MEANS TO ME

Choice is at the foundation of commitment. The following exercise may be beneficial to help you raise your awareness of what's involved in the choice to commit or not, and its attendant consequences.

1. Notice that you have the choice to make a commitment to your partner. Imagine the consequences of making it.
2. Notice that you have the choice to break the commitment to your partner. Imagine the consequences of breaking it.

Try to spend at least five minutes intending to follow each instruction. Let whatever may occur in your mind or emotions as a result of trying to follow the instructions surface. Observe your reactions. Repeat the exercise for as long and as often as seems helpful.

7

EFFECTIVE COMMUNICATION

Something we were withholding made us weak

Until we found out that it was ourselves.

Robert Frost, 'The Gift Outright'

In a conscious marriage information routinely flows back and forth between a couple. Effective communication solves problems and improves the quality of a relationship. Communication is a skill that can be learned and integrated by couples throughout the journey of their relationship.

If it were harder to get a marriage licence than a driver's licence, the divorce rate would probably drop. If every couple wishing to marry were trained in communication — or had been given relationship education at school — fewer wrecked marriages would litter the countryside. Too many marriages end in divorce simply because the wife and husband are fed up with being unable to communicate. They may not even have realised that ineffective communication was the source of their frustration.

Since relationship education is not more widely available, a couple must take responsibility for self-education to prevent poor communication from incapacitating their marriage. It is important for a couple who aspire to a functional relationship to assess their skills as a communicating team. When necessary, which is realistically almost always, they can then take steps to improve their ability to communicate. A couple who can effectively communicate will be able to undercut many problems in their relationship.

A couple might understandably expect that if they love each other, share common goals and have a commitment, their relationship would not have too many major problems. They could well be disillusioned when they continue to encounter obstacles.

Developing an effective relationship is often more challenging than a couple expect it to be: problems must be solved regularly. Communication is the primary tool available to a couple to handle their problems.

Many problems in relationships stem from ineffective communication; if there is friction, most likely communication can alleviate it. When the mortgage payment is due and there is not enough money available to pay it, this is not a relationship problem, it is an external problem. Tension between the couple about how to cope with making the payment is the problem in the relationship. Communication will not magically make money appear in the bank account; however, it will resolve the tension between the couple by creating an understanding about how the situation can be handled. Problems in relationships are often based on a lack of communication, and thus are solved by communication.

Sometimes communication is blamed for the failure of a relationship — or prescribed as the remedy — when it should not be. This is understandable since ineffective communication is the cause of many failed relationships. However, communication is not the only factor which makes a marriage work. Effective communication does solve many problems, even before they develop, yet it cannot solve everything. For example, if one spouse has not chosen to commit to the relationship and the other says something like, 'It's breaking my heart to be in an uncommitted marriage. I feel devastated'. What else can be said? Whoever it was has done a good job of communicating: no blame, to the point, authentic. Perhaps, even the uncommitted partner can articulately convey the reasons involved or anguish at the inability to make the commitment. The problem here is not communication, it is commitment. While communication should not be expected to solve all problems, it retains a central on-going role in relationships.

One of the most important tools for building a marriage is communication. Understanding the dynamics of communication will help prepare a couple to deal with many of their relationship's problems.

WHAT IT TAKES TO COMMUNICATE

Communication involves the transfer of thought between two individuals. A thought can be transferred verbally or non-verbally. Non-verbal communication includes facial expression, gesture, body language and emotion (tears, a red face, etc); it typically enhances verbal communication but cannot substitute for it. Verbal communication will always be the primary method of transferring thoughts in a relationship.

Communication is based on choice. An individual has the choice to relate or not. Attempting to communicate with someone does not ensure receptivity; it is an invitation to relate. This simple principle can save a world of frustration in a marriage. A married couple have taken on the responsibility to stay in communication. If they respect one another's personal space — if they realise and accept the fact that the other partner may not be as ready as they are to communicate at a particular moment or about a particular issue — the chances of them communicating successfully. . .when they are both ready to. . .will increase.

The most effective way to get a partner's attention is to give them your own. Attending to your partner invites them to relate. When a couple respect one another's choice to relate, communication is opened between them. Then communication can flow and accomplish the work of building understanding.

THE THREE STEPS OF COMMUNICATION

Effective communication has three steps: sending, receiving and acknowledging. To get a thought or message across the sender should be clear about what he or she says, instead of just talking words. To be receptive to the communication the other partner must be willing to know what the sender has to say. When the receiver understands the thought, he or she then acknowledges that the communication has been received. A nod or a word will do. Acknowledgment completes a cycle of communication.

Sending

To effectively communicate the sender must have a clear thought that he or she wants to have understood. It will save miscommunication and misunderstanding to do a bit of self-reflection before attempting to communicate, especially a complex or difficult thought.

A successful couple is also very comfortable with silence. Silence can help clarify thoughts, whereas a steady stream of words, confused by unclear thinking or charged with emotion, will not communicate well. Taking all day to get a clear idea of what you want to say to your partner is preferable to talking all day and saying nothing. A confused partner might take a break, go into another room or for a walk. Self-imposed pressure to perform will not help, but contemplating what really needs to be said well may. When a clear thought surfaces the sender may go on with the process of getting it across to the other.

Receiving

Another vital ingredient in the communication process involves listening. Being a good listener means being receptive, wanting to understand and having an interest in what a partner says without being judgmental. A good listener demonstrates the fact that they are taking in what's being said by giving the sender their full attention and tracking the message being communicated. A good receiver is not intrusive, but present, drawing the communication out of the sender. By simply attending to your partner while he or she is speaking you become a good receiver. Giving your attention to your partner, watching and listening as they communicate, usually involves making eye contact; however, if it is forced it will be counterproductive.

Acknowledging

A good listener is also a good acknowledger, letting the sender know that the communication has been understood. When no acknowledgment is given, sometimes a sender will continue to communicate a thought that has in fact been received. This is often frustrating for both partners. Acknowledgment can be accomplished without the receiver making a big production out of it. A nod or a smile, an 'uh-huh', or even a 'thank you' can acknowledge communication. Acknowledgment signifies understanding, not agreement. A good listener is able to acknowledge a communication with which she or he does not necessarily agree. If both partners can accept that the other person has a right to feel and think as they do, both receiving and acknowledging will be much easier on them.

The communication cycle

Sending: The sender wants the other partner to understand something.
Key: Having a clear thought about what he or she wants understood.

Receiving: The receiver is interested and wants to understand.
Key: Being receptive.

Acknowledging: The receiver lets the sender know the communication has been understood.
Key: Showing clearly that understanding has occurred.

GUIDELINES FOR EFFECTIVE COMMUNICATION

• In communication it is a courtesy, a demonstration of love, to put the other first by being willing to listen first. It is a small sacrifice, but it is a reminder of what relationship is all about.

• It is almost impossible for communication to occur in the presence of interruption; for effective communication, a couple should take turns speaking. Communication is hampered by constant interruption. Taking turns is essential. If only one partner is communicating, or dominates the interchange, effective communication will be blocked. A kitchen timer may be set, and reset, for five minutes if necessary. Of course, external interruptions can be minimised by selecting an opportune time to discuss important issues.

• In effective communication the speaker has a clear idea of the thought he or she wishes to communicate, stays on the subject and is willing to reveal him- or herself. Sometimes it is difficult to clarify your thoughts because they are about yourself! It is a risk to reveal yourself to another; but it will build trust with your partner if you can.

• Stay in contact with a partner even when he or she may be reacting unhelpfully. This is one of the most difficult aspects of communication; it can allow for the resolution of crisis situations in relationship.

• Persistence is essential for effective communication. Communication may be subverted in so many ways. A partner's feelings may be hurt at times when the other does not understand, the phone may ring, or a child may cry. There are so many distractions that it may not seem worth the effort to try again, but persistence will enable the interruptions to be overcome.

• It is the responsibility of the speaker to ensure that their communication is correctly understood. The receiver should never be blamed for not understanding; it is the sender's responsibility to complete a communication. The blame game can kill a marriage. Being critical of the receiver often stems from the sender's prior failure to get an important thought across. On the other hand, if a partner continually refuses to receive the communication, his or her commitment may be questioned. Listening is part of what both partners must do to make a marriage work.

• Completing communication cycles ensures effective communication. *Incomplete communication cycles cause dysfunction.* If too many misunderstandings build up, a relationship cannot continue to work.

Making certain that the three steps of communication — sending, receiving and acknowledging — routinely occur when a couple relate is a reliable way to monitor their communication's effectiveness. This is what a good marriage counsellor is paid to do; a couple can do it for themselves.

The purpose of these guidelines is to help couples complete communication cycles. *If you only remember one guideline — to complete communication cycles — and follow it, you can transform the patterns of communication with your partner.*

Communication guidelines

1. Be willing to listen first.
2. Take turns with your partner.
3. Don't interrupt each other.
4. Have the thought clear *before* you start speaking.
5. Stay in contact with your partner.
6. Persist with getting the thought across.
7. Take responsibility for getting your thoughts across (don't blame the receiver).
8. *Complete the communication cycle: send, receive, acknowledge.*

HOW TO IMPROVE YOUR RELATIONSHIP WITH COMMUNICATION

Understanding leads to fulfilment in marriage. Technical information about communication can be very helpful, but it is not enough. What to say, as well as how to say it, is essential for communication to be effective. *Telling your partner what you think he or she should know about you leads to an improved relationship.*

Perhaps you are worried about a problem at work and become preoccupied with it. For example, a complex project is challenging you to the limit, but you have acted more in control than you feel. The truth is that you feel inadequate. You may think telling your spouse about it would be a bother. He has his own problems. But holding the communication back about the situation at work may lead you to hold your love back too (this is what I call a 'withhold'). Perhaps your spouse will notice your preoccupation and wonder if he has done something to put you off. This kind of simple dynamic can snowball into a misunderstanding — or it can bring a couple closer together. *Communication about yourself is the key.*

Facing the risk of self-disclosure can sometimes feel like taking a step off a cliff blindfolded. Perhaps, there is something deeper than a work problem that has been at the back of your mind, something very personal. Not knowing how sensitive thoughts will be received can create an anxiety that can shut down communication. However, if you can take that first step, risk self-revelation and reach out through the anxiety to the individual you love, and tell him what you think he should know about yourself, this allows for him to be supportive of you. Maybe you will get emotional, maybe he will get emotional. Letting what's going to happen just happen is the best policy in these moments of self-doubt. It is a risk to take a relationship deeper, but it is a risk well worth taking.

Truthful communication is essential, but it must also be beneficial to the relationship. If a partner is hurt by a communication — even a truthful one — the relationship is in danger of being damaged. This is not to say a couple should tiptoe around the truth or retreat into polite platitudes. In effective communication a partner tells the truth in such a way as to not injure the other. This may be very difficult, but consideration and love, as well as an intimate knowledge of who that person is, can make it possible. It may take more than a day, in fact much longer in some instances. However, if it is something that a partner thinks should be said to the other, persistence is vital.

To tell the other what you think you should is to be forthcoming. *Being forthcoming with a partner is the ethical key to effective communication in relationship.* Self-honesty is necessary to implement this principle. If telling your partner what you think you should does not produce growth in the relationship, identifiable by a subjective sense of progress being made, self-honesty may be the impediment. Often there is a confession that should be made if there has been an interruption in the flow of communication between a couple.

Perhaps there is a noble withhold: she feels lamb roast should be served every Sunday, but hates to prepare it; he hates to eat lamb every Sunday, but thinks she enjoys serving it so doesn't mention it — twenty-five years later it comes out. Many relationships are riddled with withholds, both major and minor, that slowly sap the life from them.

BARRIERS TO COMMUNICATION

There are serious barriers to being forthcoming in relationship which can cripple communication between a couple. Many of these barriers have a noble element, as in the example about serving lamb roast on Sundays. Barriers to effective communication tend to be based on considerations a person has about how his or her partner would react to a particular communication. She wonders how he would react if she told him what she really thinks she should about their sex life, for example. It is appropriate to consider the consequences of a communication to prevent undue injury, but inappropriate to do so obsessively. A communicating partner must make his or her best judgment and go ahead. It can be damaging as well to withhold an important thought from the other. Honest communication brings issues and considerations into the light of the contact between the couple, testing their reality. Hitting the barriers to communication just as you start to take the step off the cliff can prevent you from finding out you can fly.

A common barrier to communication is fear of consequences. Fear can paralyse communication between a couple, undermining their relationship. Most often it is fear of the unknown. A couple who are communicating well almost constantly enter new territory together. This is scary, but exciting as well.

Not wanting to hurt the other's feelings can also block communication. This is a very common barrier for sensitive people, who often end up being hurt themselves by holding back. Bringing their sensitivity together with honesty will help them to break through this barrier.

Communication is sometimes withheld because an individual does not want to be thought badly of, rejected or abandoned. So many of us limit the depth of our intimacy in this way. Taking up the challenge of relationship means just going ahead and reaching out to the other anyway. The reality is that to succeed in a marriage we sometimes have to open ourselves up and say what we think and feel to our partner, regardless of the consequences.

Another barrier to communication is not taking responsibility for communicating. A person may feel the other should know without being told, perhaps giving hints or dramatising what should be said. For example, as they come to the door and his arms are full, he wants her to open the door for him and clears his throat to let her know.

Perhaps the most common of all barriers to communication and the one underlying them all is not wanting to reveal yourself — as fearful or vulnerable, or enthusiastic or delighted. This barrier cuts to the core of the psyche and, as mentioned earlier, becomes a crucial block for anyone who seriously tries to establish meaningful communication in a committed relationship. It is present in everyone and must be repeatedly faced and overcome during the lifetime of a relationship, as greater degrees of self-disclosure are

---

Barriers to communication

1. Fear of consequences.
2. Not wanting to hurt your partner's feelings.
3. Not wanting to be thought badly of or rejected.
4. Not taking responsibility for communicating.
5. *Not wanting to reveal oneself.*

---

demanded by the growth needs of the unfolding contact between the couple. Anxiety always surrounds intimate self-disclosure — honest and sensitive communication will transform it into joy.

HANDLING A COMMUNICATION CRISIS

At some point in a committed relationship, most likely at several successive points, a couple will hit a communication crisis. *In a communication crisis a couple believe they cannot go on communicating with each other.* Noticing how you subjectively feel about such a situation is an easy way to identify a crisis. If you can see a way to resolve it, you are not in a crisis. *A crisis is a situation to which no resolution can be seen.*

A communication crisis may be one manifestation of any developmental crisis in the relationship. The issue may be attraction, bonding, commitment, communication, cooperation, or a combination of these themes. In almost all crises, communication is part of the problem. In a communication crisis specifically, both partners will feel overwhelmed with having reached the limits of their ability to communicate. This is a test of a relationship. If the couple can get through the crisis rather than backing off from it, and thus failing to resolve it, their growth will continue. Furthermore, they will have succeeded as a team in making their marriage work.

To successfully resolve any crisis, including a communication crisis, involves several steps. First, you need to recognise and acknowledge that a crisis situation exists in order to empower constructive action. To know what and why it is happening — even if it is a crisis — is reassuring, whereas being in the middle of a crisis situation unawares can be disorienting and debilitating. Of course, to recognise a crisis is to admit being at a loss. Helplessness and powerlessness are the psychological hallmarks of crisis. Awareness of what the situation is and how to deal with it can enable you to overcome the intimidating nature of the experience.

Next, choosing to face the crisis makes action possible. In a crisis there is an instinctive and psychological reaction to cut and run. You may not want to face the problem; however, doing so is an unavoidable and integral part of growth.

Third, *making a conscious choice to improve the relationship with your partner is the most constructive action that can be taken in crisis — it opens a pathway through the situation.* The trick is to do it while your mind is telling you it is impossible.

Finally, by continuing to communicate, to relate, the crisis will be resolved. When a couple try to develop effective communication, it can bring on a crisis; if they continue to communicate the crisis can be resolved. In the thick of a crisis, if you continue to communicate what you think your partner should know about you, there is an excellent chance for a positive resolution.

It is not easy to get through a crisis; the situation would not have escalated to such proportions if it was. *To face a communication crisis is one of the most difficult challenges in relationship and in life.*

Resolving a crisis

1. Acknowledge that a crisis exists.
2. Choose to face the crisis.
3. Make a conscious choice to improve the relationship with your partner.
4. Continue to communicate what you think your partner should know about yourself until the crisis is resolved.

It is possible that a crisis will continue for several weeks. One way or the other, however, the crisis will resolve in time. After some weeks if the situation is truly intolerable, a separation may occur. If a couple do not have the resources to resolve the crisis, they may consciously or unconsciously agree to end their relationship, or they may stay together in a dysfunctional one.

It is a mistake to believe that it is wrong for a crisis to occur, to try to force its resolution, or to lay the blame at your partner's feet. Couples really do have limits to their ability to communicate. *Growth in relationship involves increasing the ability to communicate as a couple.* A couple should work toward crisis resolution by continuing to communicate effectively without trying to force the issue. If the partners are sincere and keep communicating, chances are that a crisis will resolve advantageously.

Effective communication increases contact, draws couples together and fulfils their relationship. In addition to its task-oriented function of keeping a relationship viable, *communication is fulfilling in and of itself.* In relationship everyone has the opportunity to be known and to know another. The willingness to be known as they really are is perhaps the greatest gift partners can give to one another.

Through communication, understanding clears away the obstacles to intimacy. When a thought is communicated, received and understood, it no longer can come between a couple. *A communicated thought vanishes as a barrier to contact between two individuals to the degree it is understood.* This is a seemingly magical process. It is the principle that underlies the salutary effects of all 'talking therapy'. A couple can make use of this principle to deepen their contact together, using a structured format which facilitates practising effective communication.

EXERCISE: COMMUNICATION DYADS

People often feel restricted in a structured format; however, a dyad structure serves as a mechanism for freeing the communication between individuals. In a dyad format, two individuals sit a comfortable distance apart, facing one another, and give their attention to each other. An accepting atmosphere prevails. The individuals do not react to one another, verbally or non-verbally. One individual gives a brief instruction to the other who responds to the instruction, while the first watches, listens and tries to understand the response to the instruction. An example of an instruction is: 'Tell me a goal you have in life.' When the response is complete, the listening partner thanks the speaking partner, acknowledging the communication.

After five minutes the roles reverse. A dyad can last up to forty minutes, with partners reversing roles every five minutes. It takes some practice to settle into the dyad format, but after the initial discomfort, smiles or giggles, two committed individuals can easily adopt the structure for the benefits it offers.

One set of three instructions given in the dyad format is known as a Relationship Evolution Dyad. The RED, as it is nicknamed, is a powerful tool for improving communication in a relationship. One partner, the listening partner, first gives the instruction, 'Tell me something you like about me', to his or her partner. The partner thinks of something that she or he likes about the other and communicates it. The partner who gave the instruction listens to the communication, tries to understand it and says 'Thank you', when it is finished. Next, the listening partner gives the instruction, 'Tell me something you think we agree on'. Once again the speaker does his or her best to respond. Again the partner who gave the instruction watches, listens and tries to understand the response and then acknowledges it. The third instruction is, 'Tell me something about yourself you think I should know', with the same listening and acknowledging occurring.

The same roles are kept by the couple for five minutes, cycling through the instructions again if time allows, and then the roles are reversed. (Timing may be by a kitchen timer or tape with chimes at five minute intervals.) The previous speaker then gives the instructions, and the cycle is followed as described above. After another five minutes the roles reverse again, and so on, until the end of about forty minutes. If the time expires in the middle of an instruction or communication, the roles reverse anyway after the listening partner thanks the speaker. This is an inconvenience, but the speaker will have another chance to get the interrupted thought across when it is his or her turn again.

During a Relationship Evolution Dyad a couple protect the semi-formality of the dyad format and intend to open up to each other to improve their relationship. The combination of structure and openness facilitates growth. At first no interruptions should be made by either partner, but after the dyad format becomes more familiar the listener may ask for clarification with the simple request, 'Please clarify that.' In the 'change-overs' some part of a communication may be lost, but it can be picked up in a later cycle.

Five minutes of a RED

Listening partner:	'Tell me something you like about me.'
Speaking partner:	'I like the way you smile when you talk about your cat.'
Listening partner:	'Thank you. Tell me something you think we agree on.'
Speaking partner:	'That the garbage has to be taken out.'
Listening partner:	'Thank you. Tell me something about yourself you think I should know.'
Speaking partner:	'Last week when we were talking about where to go on our vacation, I didn't say that I'd really rather go to the beach instead of to your parents.'
Listening partner:	'Thank you. Tell me something you like about me.'
Speaking partner:	'I like that you don't give up.'
Listening partner:	'Thank you. Tell me something you think we agree on.'
Speaking partner:	'I think we agree that we really need a vacation.'
Listening partner:	'Thank you. Tell me something about yourself you think I should know.'
Speaking partner:	'I'm really afraid my grandmother is going to die before I see her again.'

Under no circumstances should a listener correct the data his or her partner is communicating. This becomes tempting when your partner says something he or she thinks you agree on when actually you do not! However, the instruction is: 'Tell me something you *think* we agree on'. So the speaker has complied with the instruction if he or she has communicated something that, to the best of his or her judgment, is in that category.

The first two instructions set up the final instruction. The instruction 'Tell me something you like about me', is designed to increase the affinity between a couple. The instruction 'Tell me something you think we agree on', is designed to heighten the bond between the couple. The instruction 'Tell me something about yourself you think I should know', is designed to encourage self-disclosure. This final instruction provides the couple the best opportunity to deepen their contact. A RED may be considered to be successful if understanding has grown.

When the mental barriers to relationship are dissolved, sexual energy flows between the couple. The couple may even choose to disrobe and continue the RED for a while to let the contact build.

Other dyads

The dyad format may be applied with other sets of instructions than those used in the RED. Goal sharing may be practised with the following instructions, 'Tell me a goal you have in life' and 'Tell me everything I need to know to understand that goal'.

A couple can work on their commitment with the instructions, 'Tell me something a committed relationship means to you' and 'Tell me everything I need to know to understand it'. Remember, it is important to be non-judgmental when you receive your partner's communication in these dyads and to acknowledge his or her responses to the instructions.

8 CONSENSUS

He who feels punctured must once have been a bubble.

Lao Tsu

A couple who have completed the developmental tasks in the first four stages of a conscious marriage have come a long way together — and have a lot going for their relationship. They have been attracted and bonded, they have made a commitment and worked on their problems together. They have enhanced the effects of chemistry with ethical relating, they have developed common goals, they have passed through commitment and communication crises. Having succeeded to this degree, having overcome significant barriers in their relationship, the couple may well believe they have all the answers. Many relationship veterans, however, will not be surprised at this point when they find that nature has a new set of questions. In the fifth stage of a conscious marriage, the mature stage, the developmental process wants to know whether a couple will be able to really cooperate by working together consensually.

CONSENSUS IN RELATIONSHIP, MARRIAGE AND FAMILY

Cooperation, the developmental theme of mature marriage, is based on consensus. *Cooperation is working together and sharing power; consensus is two individuals choosing together, making joint decisions. Consensus serves as the means of creating cooperation in relationship.*

Consensus has begun to gain popularity in business and politics as a powerful team-building mechanism, but it has long been the foundation of good marriages. Consciously following a consensual model in marriage increases the probability of continued success as a marriage becomes a family.

A couple may begin to cooperate with one another from the early days of their relationship. If this is not the case, however, it will eventually become an issue. By the time children appear, if competitiveness has not been resolved by cooperation, the situation will become critical. What has not naturally been resolved in the development of the relationship may be intentionally resolved in the interest of the marriage's continued workability.

With consensus and cooperation the issue that is really being addressed is power in the relationship.

Changing attitudes may not have yet punctured the old patriarchal–authoritarian bubble, but they have at least dented it in the last few years. The traditional model of male dominance as the convention for dealing with power in relationship is now less valid. Certainly educated, progressive members of the community today no longer follow a paradigm of male dominance. Alternatively, female dominance might reverse the direction of abuse without offering a substantive improvement for relationship.

Some couples deal with the power issue by living parallel lives. By employing this model of marriage, couples are able to circumvent the problems that inevitably occur when partners try to work out their lives together. In parallel lives, each individual takes responsibility for their own life — exclusively. They still share a home, eat at the same dinner table, sleep in the same bed, etc — but essentially they live their lives apart from one another. Work, interests, friends, and even ideals, hopes, and fears are not necessarily shared by the partners. The parallel-lives model avoids the task of building cooperation, and the issue of power between wife and husband remains unresolved. The achievement of a balance of power between the partners is put into the 'too hard basket'.

The point is not that couples should do everything together, but that they need to find some common ground — other than the physical house they're living in — in which to share their lives if their relationship is to grow and strengthen. If they continue on as they are, one day they might just wake up and find a wall between them that's too high to scale: they won't know each other any more. Such a couple would benefit from adopting a practical approach to developing cooperation in their relationship. Just how to achieve this is discussed in the following section.

CONSENSUAL DECISION MAKING

Sharing decision making is a place to start. There are a number of areas in which the lives of couples come together that require decisions that affect both parties. Consequently, one or the other assumes responsibility for these day-to-day necessities of life. Perhaps she shops for food and he shops for the garden, perhaps she cooks and he washes up, or perhaps he cooks and she washes up. Joint decision making involves making these decisions about areas of communal responsibility *together*. A couple can start with the simpler things and work toward making consensual choices in all of the major decisions affecting their relationship.

Of course, this takes time. Indeed, the argument most often voiced against consensus is that it takes too much time. *If a couple want to have an effective marriage, they must take the time to make decisions together.* In a conscious marriage, attending to relationship does take time, at any stage. For such an approach to succeed, priorities may have to change. In the long run not only will an initial investment of time be worth it, but it can actually be expedient, given what a couple can accomplish when they work together.

For consensual decision making to be implemented a couple must learn to think in terms of *what both individuals can choose that will work.* This does not mean adopting a pattern whereby one partner makes the choice and the other gives in to it. Giving in does not necessarily involve choosing, but it may. If there is a reaction, perhaps delayed, of resentment or rebellion on the part of the partner who has given in, his or her choice was probably not involved.

Brainstorming ideas together can bring the couple together in consensual decision making. In brainstorming, a list of alternatives are creatively generated without stopping to evaluate them. Later each partner may offer their considerations about the various alternatives. Consensus will often emerge from this process, as an alternative is found that both partners can accept. It may not be either partner's first choice and may involve compromise on both parts; however, decisions that are consensually made tend to have an eerie propensity to work. The alignment of power in the relationship produces results. This is synergy at work.

Sharing authority in marriage through consensus and cooperation does not necessarily lead to an impractical amount of on-going discussion and an inefficient system — quite the opposite. As consensus is reached on various issues — money, residence, child care and education, future plans, housework, etc — a cooperative operating procedure is established to handle each situation. Who does what when, who has responsibility for a particular area, and when does the couple work together are understood and agreed upon. Such a pattern develops in any marriage: if it has been reached by consensus a cooperative atmosphere prevails in the family. *Possible battle grounds for power struggle are undercut when power is shared consensually.* The work in the family gets done instead of family time being spent on argument, thus leaving time and the predisposition for contact, play and recreation. Consensus is an important factor in harnessing the synergistic power of marriage.

ISSUES OF RESPONSIBILITY

As an on-going process consensual decision making will generate areas of responsibility for each partner. Each partner knows what he or she needs to do and has accepted responsibility for doing it. To enjoy the benefits of participating in a cooperative marriage, each partner makes the contribution necessary to support the arrangement. The responsibilities consciously undertaken to preserve the functioning of the household could be thought of as family duty. Consciously, intentionally for the good of the relationship and family, each partner assumes an obligation to something beyond personal wishes. Family duty is about a couple cooperating in the relationship's mature stage. It establishes power sharing and mutual responsibility between the couple and offers a model for teaching responsibility to the children. The best

101

way to teach children is by example; one of the most important things to teach them is responsibility.

Perhaps such a system for sharing responsibilities sounds too idealistic. It has been well documented that if both parents work, mothers bear a disproportionate share of household duties. What if one partner is more powerful than the other and subtly dominates the consensual system? These are valid concerns about the consensual family responsibility model. While such a cooperative system is an ideal to be worked toward, a couple consciously attending to the power issue in their relationship *can* increase cooperation in their marriage. A system by nature is in constant flux and self-regulation.

Mutual choice

In a conscious marriage the couple learn to make decisions together, allowing them to cooperatively share power in their relationship. A consensual decision is based on what both individuals can choose that will work. Consensual decision making creates areas of responsibility for each partner when both take responsibility for making their marriage work.

The mechanism of family responsibility relies on honest feedback and self-inspection within the couple. Each partner chooses what he or she would do to contribute to the operation of the family. *Self-responsibility is the key.* Husband and wife, based on their interests, abilities and consciences, each determine what contribution they will make. However, *mutual responsibility is also key.* Each partner, in addition to deciding what she or he will contribute to the family duties, states what he or she considers to be the other partner's duty as well.

This does not mean the couple should try to manipulate one

another with guilt, jockeying for position and seeking to control a situation. This will happen to some extent without either partner trying! Nevertheless, for the feedback to prove effective, each partner must honestly declare what he or she judges the other's responsibility in the family to be. This is a deceptively influential thing to state. So often such considerations are withheld in relationship or become the content of browbeating or nagging, neither of which has the simple power directly communicating them has. In light of the feedback, both partners again contemplate what their duties, their family responsibility, is to be. This feedback mechanism should be used periodically to ensure that responsibilities of the family are met, from paying the bills or taking out the rubbish, to having sex.

If the system is followed as described it may occur, for example, that one week the rubbish is not taken out. He has said that his duty is to cut the grass, as the garden is generally his sphere of influence. However, he has also said that since the kitchen is her job, the rubbish is hers also. She concurs that she should have ultimate say over the kitchen and that the garden is his job, however, she sees it as his responsibility to take out the garbage. So rubbish pick-up day approaches and passes, and the rubbish stays under the sink. The garden clippings go, but the garbage stays. She wonders if the family shouldn't start composting organic waste. He agrees. She offers to take care of it and he offers to take care of the rest of the rubbish. When the next pick-up day comes around, the bags are on the curb — fewer of them in fact — and the compost pile has begun.

If a couple do actually want to cooperate, an agreement is usually discovered that both can choose. As these little (or big) crises are passed a couple become more confident that such a system is workable. Whether it is spoken of openly or not, the couple has chosen to resolve the power issue between them by sharing power. The mechanism is joint decision making; that is, choosing arrangements together that work for both.

SHOULD A CONSCIOUS MARRIAGE INCLUDE CHILDREN?

At some point every couple face the question: 'Should our marriage include children?' It is not an easy question to answer. Couples sometimes have mixed feelings about it — both as a couple and as individuals. Sometimes partners' ambivalence is polarised — one is for, the other, against — when they both actually have mixed feelings; meanwhile the biological clock ticks on, and the question doesn't go away.

Brooke and Ted's next adventure

Understandably, a couple can become very comfortable at the mature stage of their relationship — with success. Having structured a marriage around love, common goals, a solid commitment and a functioning communication system, the couple may experience a satisfaction they are reluctant to risk on the unknowns of having and raising a child. Perhaps they enjoy a budget that's in the black and have two beautiful cats. Kids are expensive, and certainly require more attention than cleaning out the litter box, Ted argues. Faced with this scenario, Brooke astutely confronts a recalcitrant — but comfortable — Ted with the comment 'The cats are getting bored, Ted'.

Faced with stasis or change, many couples find they are ready to meet the next challenge.

Conscious marriage suggests a new framework within which marriage may be restructured, an approach facilitating the transformation of marriage from a tired, dysfunctional institution into a conscious, workable enterprise. Such an approach to marriage includes a provision for having and raising children. Although a couple can have a conscious marriage without having children, the model does have a bias in favour of children — not based on traditional beliefs but on pragmatic reasons. Having children can be one of the most fulfilling experiences in life. It can strengthen the marital bond and it often fulfils a deep biological imperative. Having children is one of the primary manifestations of the synergistic power of marriage.

As a marriage proceeds, the desire to have and raise children will most likely emerge. Having children is biologically where falling in love leads, and is a convincing reason to commit to a relationship. Having children can be an expression of synergy naturally arising in the unfolding of the contact between two individuals in a conscious marriage. Consciously entering the flow of marital synergy can empower, direct and deepen meaning for a couple in a way the traditional and counter-traditional approaches cannot match. A couple choosing to conceive a child is a powerful event. An alignment of intention and a readiness to enter the next stage of their marriage ensures a continued workability and cooperative atmosphere for the marriage.

Children and responsibility

A couple who may have spent some time building their relationship — forging a bond, making a commitment, and establishing effective communication — will probably find their relationship experiences new stresses with the birth of their first child. No advice, no book, no amount of forethought can prepare a couple for what it will really be like when their marriage becomes a family. Demands of added responsibility on both partners can burden their relationship, especially if they become too complacent in their comfortable marriage. A crisis of cooperation is precipitated which can be highly disorganising to the new family. The work load is increased. Time is redistributed. Focuses shift and the relationship may be shaken or temporarily break down. A successful resolution of the crisis will effect a restructured relationship, incorporating new consensual agreements, featuring major changes to previous routines.

THE SYNERGISTIC POWER OF MARRIAGE

Whether a couple manage to mature on their own in their

relationship by cooperating through consensus and compromise, or whether they achieve this in the context of having a child, their marriage will benefit in many ways from having done so. The effects of marital synergy are palpable.

When the developmental task of cooperation has been accomplished — in addition to the ones of attraction, bonding, commitment and effective communication which precede it — a couple may not even know why, but they will feel a rewarding sense of achievement. Not only will they feel a sense of contentment and fulfilment with their relationship and family life: marital synergy has an almost preternatural capacity to generalise, creating a tendency for a couple to find themselves succeeding in reaching goals outside the marriage. This seems to occur for individual goals as well as shared ones, at least if they are realistic. Concerns about finances, where to live, profession and so on seem to be taken care of by the couple without the struggle characteristic of a relationship's early days. Perhaps this is because through alignment a couple can focus their power to constructive ends rather than directing it to cross-purposes.

The old patriarchal adage proclaimed that behind every successful man is a good woman. Today's couples who constructively share power in their relationship may find new vistas of accomplishment await those who are behind each other in a conscious marriage.

EXERCISE: FAMILY RESPONSIBILITY BY CONSENSUS

Step 1: Together a couple generate a list of responsibilities that need to be shared between them

Step 2: A brainstorming session can be conducted to generate possible ways of dealing with each area of responsibility. Ideas should be allowed to flow freely, uninterrupted by judgments, and written down.

Step 3: Both partners contemplate what they would like to do, can do, and are willing to do that is on the list of responsibilities, list those duties and discuss them.

Step 4: Having understood what the other partner considers as his or her own responsibility, each partner then lists what he or she considers to be the other's duty and communicates it to him or her.

Step 5: In light of the other partner's considerations, each partner again contemplates what his or her own family duty should be and shares the results with his or her partner.

Step 6: Steps 4 and 5 should be repeated periodically as needed.

9 HELP FOR AN AILING MARRIAGE

I have nothing to offer but blood, toil, tears and sweat.

Winston Churchill

Relationship is such a complicated matter, especially when it goes awry, that it is often difficult to understand what has gone wrong, much less what could be done to set it right. If you are caught up in the tumult of a crisis with a partner, objectivity can be hard to come by. During difficulties couples will use the tools at hand — often the same ones that have not prevented the upset — or perhaps revert to destructive behaviour, which will not resolve it. The raised voice, the slammed door, the sullen silence and worse mark the terrain of an embattled relationship. Suffering is so common for couples, but it does not have to be.

WHERE TO START: PREVENTING VIOLENCE

Physical violence, of course, is the worst case scenario for a domestic argument, and, unhappily, not the least frequent. Typically, insufficient skills to cope with problems frustrate a couple, leading them toward violent behaviour. Poor communication skills, coupled with a low ability to control angry and violent impulses, is usually the toxic mixture that erupts into violence. Quite simply, *if violence is occurring in a relationship it should be stopped.* Skills cannot be built, nor a relationship rebuilt, amid continued destructiveness. If a couple cannot break a violent

---

Fighting does not solve problems!

---

pattern, they can separate for an hour, a day, a week, for however long it takes, or forever.

One of the most useful rules in relationship is *walk away from a fight*. Fighting — verbal, emotional or physical, and usually in uncontrollable combination — will not help solve problems between a couple. It will exacerbate them. In the light of calm reflection this may seem obvious; however, in the potentially explosive atmosphere of intense emotional interchange, a couple can rapidly forget it. Individuals at the end of their repertoire of coping strategies may subconsciously start a fight to reduce tension or to offer an escape route from a failing relationship. Rarely will a couple be able to fight in such a way that damage is not done to the relationship. Most partners feel guilty at the injury they do during a fight, and psychologically, if not physically, withdraw from the relationship as a result. If a couple having problems wish to realistically address them, fighting must first be stopped. It might not be easy, but it is essential. The Hippocratic injunction is applicable here: first do no harm. Before a couple can expect to heal their ailing relationship, they must first stop making it worse by fighting.

After a certain point in every brewing fight, events escalate out of control. This is the control point. Before the control point passes, the couple can stop the fight — the trick is to do just that because after passing it, it is easy to be automatically swept toward destruction. One or both partners can lose effective control, and say and do things that are later regretted. A technique on how to avoid doing this, and how to walk away from a fight before passing the control point, is given at the end of this chapter.

DIAGNOSING RELATIONSHIP PROBLEMS

If a couple can become aware of which key factor or factors are absent from their relationship, they can determine the appropriate approach for making improvements. Effort is often wasted by couples and counsellors addressing an area of a relationship which is not the source of the problem. Perhaps a therapist who is an expert in emotional release will encourage a couple to express their feelings when the problem is really commitment; or a couple who believe communication solves all problems will inflame their power struggle by talking at cross-purposes — and later fighting — when they need to focus on cooperation. Many couples need help not only with solving their problems, but in accurately identifying them. Chemistry, common goals, commitment, communication and consensus occupy cardinal points on the map to guide a troubled couple out of difficulties.

Embarrassingly enough, at one time or another we all have found ourselves in the role of the apprentice mechanic who was discovered pounding mindlessly on an engine block with a hammer. 'Need a wrench for that job, don't you?', dryly enquired the boss. 'Yes,' replied the apprentice, 'I know, but it's lost'. So many relationships are battered like the apprentice's motor, both of which could be repaired with the correct tool.

Identifying and solving problems

Finding out what is wrong in a relationship can be accomplished by identifying which factor or factors are missing. The Five Cs of conscious marriage help to make a relationship work if they are present. If one or more are absent, the relationship has characteristic problems based on what is missing. A couple can improve their relationship by understanding which factor or factors are absent, and by using the right techniques to solve their particular problems.

No amount of communication can create attraction if chemistry's spark is not there. Talking — or shouting — about shared goals will never allow them to develop. Talking cannot force a choice to commit. A couple yelling at the top of their lungs are not communicating. If the will to power is entrenched, no well-reasoned argument, no matter how loudly voiced, will displace it. A relationship cannot be verbally forced into shape when its development has been arrested. Repeated attempts to do so only make matters worse. *For meaningful change to occur in a relationship both individuals must want change and choose to participate in the process.* Understanding where the problem lies can help a couple to avoid fruitless efforts at improvement and realistically match the help to the kind of problem they have. Then the growth and development of their relationship can resume.

FIVE PROBLEM SCENARIOS

The following scenarios introduce five types of problem marriages. Each type suffers from the absence of one of the Five Cs that make a conscious marriage work. These scenarios accentuate the features of each type; they are not case histories. The types do actually describe how *some* couples think, feel and behave. However, these couples are the pure type. Usually relationships are not so clear cut. Most real couples have some similarity to *all* of the types from time to time. The types are not meant to reduce the richness and complexity of real couples' lives to caricature. They are for helping couples to identify and solve their problems.

Couple A

On the surface all seems in place in the lives of Couple A: house, profession and child. Couple A present an almost perfect picture of married life: order, time spent relating, concern for the child, attention to detail. Couple A take pride in 'working on their relationship' and have mapped out their life together. They share goals, have committed to the relationship and can effectively communicate.

After knowing Couple A for a while an observer may begin to suspect that their life together seems a bit too perfect. Friends notice they have difficulty getting personally close to either partner. They are surprised to encounter subtle opposition or sabotage of their friendship with one partner by the other. It is almost as if friendship poses a threat to the marriage. Hidden beneath the social veneer, Couple A's 'orderly' life is punctuated with upsets, arguments and seemingly more than their share of crises. Couple A's boy seems happy, but on closer inspection the happiness seems artificial. Learning problems at school develop, and a teacher expresses concern to Couple A, who reassure the teacher, emphasising how hard they work at being a good family. After seven years of marriage, Mr A falls in love with a co-worker, and Couple A is plunged into a terminal crisis. Conflict intensifies between the couple as Mr A refuses to give up his 'relationship' and Mrs A demands it. The marriage deteriorates, violent scenes emerge, and after a few painful months Mr A finally moves out of the house. In a year he files for divorce.

What happened to this apparently well-adjusted couple? Couple A were never in love. They had talked themselves into the relationship; it was not attraction that had brought them together. Chemistry never entered into Couple A's relationship. Missing out on the chemistry at the start precludes romantic love as an attractive force ever really working for the couple. Mentally oriented and wilful, Couple A were able to construct the edifice of a life together according to a plan by force of will. Unfortunately it was built on sand. The underlying insecurity of their lovelessness was at the root of their reluctance to make close friends of others, as well as their son's problems. In a couple who have never had chemistry, attraction does not maintain the union as it should. Disagreement tends to erupt into chaotic conflict, causing more injury than if chemistry had been present from the beginning of the relationship. The great danger for this type of marriage is that one of the partners *will* fall in love, shattering the marriage along its fatal flaw.

Fortunately, the Type A marriage is not common. It has been included to give a comprehensive picture of the problems possible in relationship. However, many couples, whether they have fallen out of love or are going through a rocky period, sometimes assume its characteristics: it is not uncommon for couples to treat each other carelessly from time to time. Since their marriage is not based on chemistry, a pure Type A couple have a less than optimistic prognosis. Romantic love cannot be made to happen by a couple or a marriage counsellor. Marriage counselling would be a waste of time for all involved if Mr A, having fallen in love, is committed to his new relationship. Optimally, couples with periodic Type A symptoms, should choose to accept and adjust to their situation. No marriage is always ideal. Acknowledging this reality will help most couples. Nevertheless, a couple with Type A tendencies will need to monitor themselves to guard against the potential for ill-treatment in a loveless relationship. Adopting an ethical system would probably help them more than anything else. However, problems along the lines described might still come up.

Couple B

Couple B fell in love while on vacation, planned a wonderful life together and were married in three months. They conceived a child almost immediately and built a home together. They were overjoyed at their good fortune and proud of their achievement. However, Couple B were of markedly different personalities. She was introverted, bookish and prone to be a 'stay-at-home', while he was extroverted, voluble and sociable. Mrs B's friends were initially delighted that she had found someone, they had privately doubted she ever would, and hoped the sociable Mr B would bring her out of her shell. It was not to be. Following the birth of their first child, it seemed she became even more withdrawn and was increasingly found virtually hiding behind a book. He was at first mildly put off by his wife's distant style, but did not dwell on the problem and quickly found himself involved in activities he had enjoyed prior to the marriage: sports, outings and socialising. Over the next three years Couple B gradually drifted apart and their love faded. On one of Mr B's outings he was attracted to another woman, and as she shared his social circle and sports interests, they were together often. Finally they had to admit their involvement to themselves and to their friends, to whom it had been obvious for some time. Mrs B was crushed in a quiet, sad sort of way, and withdrew even more. Mr B continued his relationship for some months. The young woman eventually fell in love with someone else and broke off with Mr B, but the damage had been done. The couple made efforts to stay together for their child's sake, but several months later, Mr B, feeling suffocated, could stand it no longer and moved out of the house.

Couple B lacked common goals to begin with and never developed any. Their romantic courtship and love affair had enough momentum to carry them into a relationship which lacked this crucial factor, but their personality differences became highlighted by having little shared direction. Their bond was too weak. Sadly, a child in common was not enough to keep them together. In a couple whose personalities were more compatible, the child would have probably been enough to sustain a bond. However, Couple B didn't fit together so they couldn't stick together. While Couple B did in fact love each other, that love was not cemented by the bond of common goals.

Couple B's situation is a heart-breaking one. The forces pulling the relationship apart were just greater than those holding it together. Inexorably, the couple were drawn apart and were not able or willing to prevent it. A great many marriages that fail, do so for this reason. It is often an agonising process; perhaps there are repeated separations and reconciliations.

A Type B couple may have made a commitment to each other, but it is undermined by weak common goals. While the couple's future prognosis is not as bleak as that of the Type A marriage, it must be a guarded one. There is the opportunity that with support and help, a Type B couple can grow together instead of apart by emphasising areas of common interest. A Type B couple can also develop common goals, but it takes work. Communication can be used as a tool to build and deepen contact between the couple. If a couple's interests and personalities are not too far apart, common goals, like children, professional interests and future plans can strengthen their bond enough for them to make it. In this case, however, Mr B probably would never be able to develop an interest in books, while Mrs B would always feel uncomfortable at sporting or social events. Nonetheless, a Type B couple can salvage their marriage if they are motivated to do so by nurturing their love and commitment and working on forging a lasting bond.

Couple C

Instantly interested in one another, Couple C fell in love; it was an intense relationship from the beginning. Similar in background and personality, Couple C got married because they both really wanted to have children. This they did with dispatch, producing a daughter and a son in less than three years. Couple C appeared to have the ingredients for an enduring relationship and a full family life; however, the union was marred by jealousy.

The vivacious and flirtatious Mrs C had left a previous relationship to enter the marriage. Mr C, articulate and socially gregarious, had a roving eye himself, and during the period after the second child was born had an affair while out of town on business. Always intense, Couple C's relationship had become increasingly fractious, and the affair pushed it into violent verbal argument. Mr C was concerned about having had an affair. He acknowledged that it did seem to indicate a problem, but in Mrs C's estimation, he had not adequately repented. It was at about this time that their son began to be reported for a series of behavioural problems at school: bullying, fighting and classroom disruptiveness. Couple C seemed to get into heated arguments every other month over what should be done with him following the latest incident. Mr C was soon discovered to have indulged in another sexual fling, and this was the last straw for Mrs C, who promptly moved out with the two children into her mother's house. Mr C, at first surprised, was in a few weeks depressed. It weighed heavily upon both partners that they had brought two children into the world and were now failing to provide a home for them. They arranged a reconciliation — Mrs C became pregnant with their third child even before she moved back into their home.

During the next eighteen months, which saw the birth of another daughter, the couple slipped back into a pattern of argument and division. More and more they seemed to go their own ways, he spending his time in business, she homemaking and raising the three children. The next affair he had, Mr C determined Mrs C would not discover it. However, when Mrs C became involved in a sexual relationship with a friend of the family, partially out of loneliness and partially for revenge, she made it no secret. Mrs C's love affair led to a violent confrontation that made previous fights seem tame. After admitting her revenge motive to Mr C, and how guilty she felt about what she had done, Mrs C broke off her extramarital relationship. The couple decided to enter counselling and worked on communicating, but after several sessions stopped. The counselling did not seem to help.

Couple C stumbled on together for another year during which Mr C feared having another affair, and his business suffered from worry. Mrs C sought help privately and began to grow as an individual, learning how to cope with Mr C without the destructive arguments. Mr C also began to mature and the marriage entered a period of growth that saw more harmony in the family. There were still problems and upsets, but the relationship had improved and was better able to cope with them. There were no more affairs and the son's behavioural problems unexpectedly disappeared.

What had been the problem? How was it solved? Why didn't the counselling really help? It should be no mystery that Couple C's relationship suffered from a failure of commitment. In a relationship of this type the prognosis is a toss up: the future could go either way. As easily as the problem was cleared up in this scenario, it could have continued as it had for ten years, destroying the marriage and family. Indeed, many relationships of this type end in tragedy of one variety or another, without the couple ever becoming aware of how to address the core issue. They may even misdiagnose their problem. Often a couple will believe the problem is 'space' or freedom or tolerance. The chronic philanderer may honestly hold the conviction that if his spouse was just more open-minded the marriage would be all right! It is also common in the Type C relationship that the couple really do know what the issue is, but have made a silent contract not to face it.

The success of the Type C couple's relationship boils down to their choice to commit to the marriage. In the case of Couple C, the marital problems, which were beyond their capacity to address, were caused by a lack of commitment. As many well-meaning couples discover, chemistry and compatibility are not enough to make a marriage work. Couple C was not helped by counselling aimed at improving communication because they could already communicate! What helped their relationship was for both individuals to exercise their power of choice to be committed to each other. In a way they stumbled onto it; many couples do not. Couple C sincerely wanted their marriage to work; they loved their children, each other, and they chose to make it work. It is a powerful circumstance to have such ability, recognise it, and exercise it.

Couple D

Generally this book follows a growth and development approach. By the same process that clinical patients get well in psychotherapy, normal people grow and develop. Barriers to growth, developmental crises and environmental variables all affect the process of growth. Sometimes intervention is desirable by a paid practitioner, minister, or social service agency at times of crisis or when seemingly impassable barriers are encountered.

The Type D marriage is probably the most frequent user of these services, and rightly so. Marriage counsellors and family therapists regularly treat Type D couples and families and can often help them. Communication problems are their central issue, and counselling techniques have been largely designed to promote communication. The outlook for a Type D couple is probably better than for any other, especially if intervention comes early. Chemistry, common goals and a committed relationship are strong predictors of success in marriage.

If a couple cannot adequately communicate, and have not learned to do so, professional help can be indispensable to the marriage's future. There are many variations in personality and the nature of obstacles in Type D couples, but they all have the common complaint of dysfunctional communication and, in the absence of counselling, do not have a good prognosis for handling the problem. Of course, motivation is always an issue. How many psychologists does it take to change a light bulb? Only one, but the light bulb has to want to be changed. Type D couples are often motivated by love and commitment to help themselves, or to seek out professional assistance.

Mr D was born on a farm, and was raised by strict, taciturn parents. Mrs D was shy as a child and did not have much of a social life until she attended university, met Mr D and fell in love with him. They both wanted to get married, raise children and settle in the suburbs. They were committed to their family, which grew as a boy and then a girl were born within four-and-a-half years. Mr D worked hard to provide for the family whom he loved dearly, but he had trouble relaxing. Mrs D became involved with charities and social groups to vary the routine of child care and housework. Though still in love, Couple D had problems with their sex life. They secretly doubted that it was really proper to discuss such matters, and both felt guilty, thinking they were just being selfish.

Mrs D eventually discussed the problem with a girlfriend, who invited her to join a women's group. At first very reluctant to do so, Mrs D eventually began attending the group — in several months it changed her life. She was excited to know that people did talk about sex as well as other aspects of their lives; she bloomed and became increasingly active in women's issues. Mr D was glad to see his wife become more interested and involved in life, but felt threatened by the women's group and silently hurt that she could share an intimacy with her women friends that she could not share with him. He gradually increased his after-dinner alcohol intake and silently moped around the house. Any approach Mrs D made to draw him out seemed to cause only embarrassment, driving him further away. It occurred to Mrs D to leave her husband, as some of her friends had done, but she was thrown into crisis realising she really loved him, valued their family and could not leave him. Finally she approached their minister, Mr D's sometime golf partner, in desperation and sobbed out her dilemma. The minister was very supportive, comforted Mrs D and promised to talk to her husband. The next time they played golf, the minister kindly but directly told Mr D of his wife's consternation, sensing that, although he was embarrassed, Mr D's good heart and dedication to his family would prevail when marriage counselling was recommended.

Couple D attended marriage counselling and Mr D sat in stolid silence through two sessions, a sheen of sweat at times visible on his forehead, as he listened to his wife and the counsellor chat, slowly beginning to discuss the issues in the marriage. Following each session, Mr D resolved he would not return to another. During the third session Mr D began to tremble and tears began to roll down his face. Finally he said to his wife in a hoarse whisper, 'I've never even told you how much I love you'. Neither the counsellor nor Mrs D pushed him, and gradually Mr D began to talk about himself and the relationship over the next few sessions. In two months the relationship between Couple D was relieved from years of built up tension. In the eighth session the D's were talking about breaking off the counselling as they had made so much progress, when the counsellor brought up the topic of sex, and a curtain of silence dropped. It was like starting the process all over again, but this time it was easier, and in four more weeks the counsellor ended the sessions with the couple's agreement. Their life together had changed, including their ability to talk about sex. They still had problems, Mr D was still at times taciturn and distant and Mrs D was still at times frustrated, but now they were able to deal with problems themselves.

The Ds are typical of so many couples who have communication problems. They had grown up in families where communication skills were not modelled — rather, where barriers to communication had become institutionalised and were passed on. Couple D did not really have a sexual problem but a communication one due to their inability to discuss the subject. Their guilt arose from having withheld things from each other that should have been discussed, not from sexual hangups. Mrs D, with help, conquered her own problems as many women do, whereas Mr D had a tougher time overcoming his barrier to communication. He actually went through the barrier — suppressed emotions in his case — in the third counselling session and was able to express himself adequately thereafter. Three factors — his willingness to face the crisis, his wife's patience and understanding, and the counsellor's skill — allowed this to happen.

How many Type D couples are as fortunate? How many men shrink away from the unknown challenges of really relating? How many wives show the patience and perseverance and have the love and commitment to endure the process? How many counsellors have the knack to help a couple through a crisis of this sort? Many couples with communication problems do not make it. With Type D couples it is particularly sad when they do not because they have so much going for them. However, communication problems place great stress on a couple's commitment, and the strain is often too great. The love between a couple is only so strong, the bond of common goals of limited value and commitment too often a fickle reality.

Couple E

Couple E had it all, almost. Mr E was already a successful businessman when he met and fell deeply in love with his younger wife-to-be. He was the son of conventional, small-town parents and had acquired some of his father's male chauvinism. She was the only child of ethnic parents; her father was authoritarian and had emotionally dominated the family. Couple E had a romantic courtship and an exciting sex life. Both wanted the good life: home, a large family, and an active social and cultural involvement, which Mr E's success was able to materially provide. Both were bright, articulate and worked hard to achieve their common goals. In the first twelve years of marriage Couple E had six children, three boys and three girls. Mr E had opportunities for extramarital relationships, but he always declined since he was very committed to his wife. Mrs E poured her energy into the children, home and family business.

As the years passed, the intensity of Couple E's relationship was more prone to argument than sexual activity, although they were fond of giving the impression, which was accurate, of an active sex life. Couple E would argue heatedly over what seemed irrelevant things: the shortest route to the airport, how to make an omelette, or how to play a hand of cards. The issue was always the same: who knew best, who was right, who would win. Couple E's competitiveness, which had been channelled into the office and children, became a problem as the children approached young adulthood and the family's financial position was secure.

There had always been a power struggle of sorts between Couple E: he used his status of successful breadwinner to get his way, while she used her sexuality to get hers. When the children left home to attend uiversity, Couple E's problems were highlighted as they were forced to spend more time together. Finally, Mrs E, in her fifties, opened a real estate office which became quite successful. This was perceived as a threat by Mr E whose position as the sole provider was undercut. He became depressed and sought help from a psychoanalyst. The depression — it turned out — was rooted in suppressed anger at his wife. It came as no real surprise to him two years later when he discovered evidence that Mrs E was engaged in an extramarital affair; however, it was devastating to him and the relationship nonetheless. After nearly thirty years of marriage the Es were divorced.

Couple E had passed through the first four stages of development of their relationship only to be blocked in the fifth: the mature stage. They were defeated by their compulsion to win. The power struggle was never resolved by Couple E, as they continued to vie for the upper hand even when it threatened to destroy their marriage. Each had made huge sacrifices for the good of the relationship and family, but was unable to give up the desire for ultimate authority. Both shared chemistry, goals, commitment and effective communication, but were unable to share power in their relationship — thus destroying all that they had shared.

Ironically, Couple E did cooperate on building a home, family and business, but were unable to adjust to living as equals when the children left home. They did try to overcome the power issue, and succeeded to a degree, but were finally unable to complete the developmental task of achieving cooperation in their relationship. Mr E's chauvinism clashed with Mrs E's life-long rebellion against her father's domination. The competence of both — effectiveness in work, homemaking and parenting — was perceived as a challenge by the other, leading to the chronic fights and disagreements which increased in frequency and fervour as the years passed. It would have taken a strong and astute therapist to confront the E's with their problem, but the opportunity never arose. In a way, with all their accomplishments, they were too proud to receive help as a couple. They had built their own life together and they were destined to tear it down.

Type E couples face the developmental challenge of sharing power in relationship. Having achieved a degree of success in their lives and relationship, Type E couples are often effective, high-powered and competitive. In this respect, their success can serve as the foundation of their failure, as Couple E demonstrated. The prognosis for a Type E couple accomplishing shared power may not be as gloomy as Couple E's experience suggests. Many Type E couples are able to delineate areas of responsibility consensually in which each has authority, as well as duty. Perhaps if Mrs E had been able to begin working five or ten years earlier it would have made a difference. But, more than likely, Mr E would not have approved.

In any event, compromise is a skill Type E couples must develop in order to learn to cooperate. Couple E always saw compromise as defeat. To communicate is one necessary factor in compromise, but *to be willing to be affected by the other's communication and adjust accordingly for the good of the relationship is crucial.* This is a quality that is hard to learn if it is not present. It comes from love.

While Couple E did love one another, their love was eroded by time and dissension. While they were able to compromise on behalf of the business and the children's welfare, they were ultimately unable to compromise for each other. Cooperation is the last crucial challenge of love in a relationship. Type E couples who achieve it have a surplus of love at the final crisis.

FIVE WAYS TO FAIL, FIVE WAYS TO SUCCEED

To have a fully developed conscious marriage all of the basic factors must be present: chemistry, common goals, commitment, communication, and consensus. When one or more of the factors are missing, the relationship will be unfulfilled in varying degrees.

The Type A, or loveless, marriage is an artificial relationship offering little promise of satisfaction. The Type B, or directionless, marriage is characterised by love without compatibility; it lacks cohesion. The Type C, or uncommitted, relationship stands at the juncture separating a relationship from a marriage; if a commitment is not made to the relationship an actual marriage is never created. The Type D, or dysfunctional, marriage has the basic factors to form a marriage, without the factor of effective communication which is ultimately needed to make it work. The Type E, or competitive, marriage can function, providing some fulfilment to a couple, but it is incomplete in that the power issue between the couple remains unresolved. The addition of each successive factor gives more vitality to a relationship, increasing the level of a couple's satisfaction and fulfilment.

HELP FOR AILING MARRIAGES

As mentioned, to improve a problem-plagued relationship, a couple need to know what is causing their problems, then appropriate helping strategies can be brought to bear. The nature of a couple's problems gives hints about the factors causing them and how to focus help accurately.

Type A marriages are relatively rare and can be hard to identify. In a pure Type A marriage, nothing will really work in the relationship, although the couple may have convinced themselves — and their acquaintances — that it does. The relationship may appear orderly on the surface but feel hollow within. The lack of love in the Type A couple will be reflected in how carelessly the couple treat each other. Type A couples often fail to respond to each other on the human level, sometimes disregarding simple requests, or more important ones. In fact, they may ignore one another's pain while pretending all is well. The worst Type A couples can become violent, although friends may never be told of the chaos behind the facade, and its discovery may shock them. Feelings of anxiety, insecurity and instability will probably surround the Type A couple, even if a social veneer of order covers it. Type A marriages have been known to have children as part of the pretence. If children are present they may be insecure, behave artificially, or in other ways act out the family's internal problems.

Type B marriages characteristically lack purpose and cohesion, a sense of togetherness. The couple may sound vague on the subject of what their life together is all about. The husband and wife follow separate interests to the exclusion of coming together in the pursuit of common goals. Perhaps they are of different personality makeup, but do not seem to complement one another in forming a couple.

Type C marriages tend to demonstrate dramatic signs of their lack of commitment, such as infidelity, frequent and destructive fights or emotional displays, and a lack of family unity. These problems don't go away, but intensify over time. The couple may seem oblivious to the fact that they even have a problem, or totally deny it.

Type D marriages have communication problems in addition to chemistry, common purpose and commitment. The couple may complain of tension, frustration and guilt, but still have the motivation to make their marriage work. Common signs of withheld communication, including

Five types of ailing marriages

	Absent factor	Symptoms	Diagnosis	Treatment	Prognosis
Type A	Chemistry	Partners don't have real friends; abusiveness; unresponsiveness; tendency to fall in love extramaritally; masked insecurity	Loveless	Introduce ethics and adjust to lowered expectations	Guarded
Type B	Common goals	Incompatibility; lack of cohesion; directionlessness	Directionless	Draw out and emphasise common goals	Fair
Type C	Commitment	Drama; arguments/ fights; infidelity; denial of problem	Uncommitted	Acknowledge lack of commitment as the problem; make a commitment	Poor/good
Type D	Communication	Frustration; guilt/ criticalness; withholding of information; tension	Dysfunctional	Improve ability to communicate	Fair/good with counselling
Type E	Consensus	Competitiveness; manipulation; longstanding conflict; power struggle	Competitive	Give up the power struggle; learn and use consensus building skills	Fair

criticalness of the partner, may also be present.

Type E marriages often will show signs of success in relationship and life: financial success, children and home. However, a power struggle will also be evident. Competitiveness, manipulation and longstanding conflict signal the Type E relationship.

The different types of ailing marriages can be improved by aiming help at the factors causing their basic problems.

Help for Type As

Type A marriages were more common in the days when couples did not as often marry out of free choice. Of the five types, Type A is the most difficult to improve because when love is absent neither the couple themselves nor a helper can change that fact. *Adopting and following an ethical system can really help a Type A couple.* Non-injury, truthfulness and honesty can bring their actual behaviour towards one another closer to their ideal. Also, accepting the inherent limitations of a Type A marriage and adapting to the situation that exists, can make the couple happier together.

The strength of a couple's investment in holding to their pretence of a good relationship will determine whether change is possible or not. Perhaps the couple firmly believe they already treat one another well — despite convincing evidence to the contrary — so they don't think they need an ethical system. There are well-adjusted Type A couples, but if they consider their lives fulfilling, their relationship will not be the source. It would be humbling for a Type A couple to admit that the reality of their relationship does not match their high ideal for it. Nonetheless, it would be better for the couple to face the reality.

It is always the choice of a couple to stay together or to separate. A Type A couple, recognising the cause of their problems, might consider the latter alternative if the relationship is not far advanced. However, if children are already involved, separation may not be indicated. The presence of offspring in a Type A marriage will add love to the family, perhaps enough to keep the couple together. Type A couples can be friends, treat one another kindly and support each other interdependently. They may wish to make the best of their situation, or if they can learn from their mistakes, they may choose to move on to a more fulfilling relationship.

Help for Type Bs

Type B couples can deepen the contact between them through communication (utilising Relationship Evolution Dyads, see page 95, or counselling) allowing buried common goals to surface. Also, through goals listing (see page 66), each partner can uncover hidden goals that may be held in common with the other, and competing goals that have acted subversively between the couple to drive them apart. By becoming aware of their sources of conflict, a couple can eliminate them. Divisive goals are often neurotic — goals which are unrealistic or impossible to reach — and can be easily relinquished when identified. Important common goals, such as having children, owning a home together or having a workable relationship, can be enough to hold a couple together. *Developing, drawing out, stressing and supporting common goals will increase cohesion in a Type B couple.* Using this strategy, the couple may be able to save their marriage if it is in danger.

Tolerance for one another's personal goals can go a long way toward diffusing conflict as well. Healthy couples pursue separate interests as well as common ones, balancing personal needs with those of the relationship. A Type B couple may be able to find an agreeable balance that provides enough cohesion to unite them in common purpose, while also providing freedom of expression for each individual. To some degree this approach will help many couples who have some Type B features. Often a partner in a Type B couple will feel threatened by the other's separate goals. However, if common goals can be uncovered or accentuated to strengthen their bond, a couple can allow more leeway to the partners' individual interests. The security of the bond common goals provides offers the freedom of pursuing individual interests to each partner.

Help for Type Cs

Type C marriages can only be substantially improved by the uncommitted partner or partners committing to the relationship. This is a matter of his, her or their choice. But the couple must know the choice to commit exists before they can make it. It is often the case that Type C couples do not recognise the underlying cause of their problems, attributing their difficulties to almost anything but the real and psychologically threatening cause. These couples often collude subconsciously to deny the true nature of their problem out of fear of responsibility or commitment, or resistance to change. They may latch onto false causes and solutions while perpetuating the true cause.

Often a crisis in a Type C couple will be precipitated by one partner threatening to leave the relationship if the other does not give up extramarital sexual activity. In many cases this is not an inappropriate step. Optimally, the uncommitted partner is simply given a choice. A counsellor could be helpful in this respect, but it may be difficult to involve the straying partner in counselling sessions. It is important to remember that both partners have choice in the matter and only if both choose commitment can the relationship grow into a committed marriage. If the uncommitted partner chooses to continue being unfaithful, that choice is his or hers to make. It is also the faithful partner's choice to leave the relationship if the situation is truly intolerable.

Much of the pain and destructive drama common to Type C relationships can be avoided by calmly confronting the uncommittedness. The danger to these couples is for the offended partner to retaliate against his or her betrayal by responding in kind. Sexual revenge is a dangerous game to play. Although it can provide excitement for a bored and hurt husband or wife, it rarely leads to improvement of the relationship. In rare cases, it does shock the relationship into change, but it is highly risky, potentially leading to violence or an endless downward spiral of mutual retribution.

The downside risk of uncommittedness for Type C couples is steep and should be borne in mind as the goal of mutual choice in commitment is pursued. Since a Type C couple's relationship has been stalled by the absence of commitment, it may also lack effective communication and be prone to power struggle, creating a potentially lethal situation. A hell of betrayal, jealousy and anger can drive a Type C couple past the point of no return.

The Type C marriage will only improve if both partners make the choice to commit to each other. Help for a Type C couple is based on acknowledging and accepting this fact. Drama aimed at trying to force this choice upon a partner will hurt rather than help. If to hurt is what the couple want, the relationship would best be abandoned before it escalates out of control.

Help for Type Ds

The way to improve the relationship of a Type D couple is to regard all relationship problems as communication problems which can be solved by opening up communication. These couples have chemistry, shared goals and commitment on their side, combining to create a good prognosis for improvement. The earlier their communication problem is identified and addressed, the higher the chances of success will be.

The build up of unexpressed thoughts and feelings between a couple can weigh them down over time. Self-help communication guidelines and Relationship Evolution Dyads (see page 95) will often assist a Type D couple in establishing meaningful dialogue. If the barriers to communication are substantial, outside help is probably required. The potential tragedy for the Type D couple is for their love, common goals and commitment to be worn down by their lack of communication. Many good marriages have been destroyed by this process, without the couple ever clearly understanding what was happening to them or how they could have prevented it.

Help for Type Es

Supporting growth in a Type E couple implies resolving the power struggle in favour of cooperation. The chances of this outcome are dependent on how deeply the couple is caught up in their power struggle. If the partners are more dedicated to winning the competition than to seeing their marriage succeed, cooperation will seem like a loss to them. The couple must be motivated and willing to give up the immediate struggle or issue for the long-term sake of their relationship. In any relationship, what a couple want is usually conclusive. If they want a fulfilling relationship, then giving up ascendance for shared power can be an achievable sacrifice. If the couple are motivated, the probable outcome improves considerably. Adopting the practice of consensus building as described in Chapter 8 is the chief means for establishing cooperation in a Type E marriage. Not only must new patterns of sharing power be learned for the relationship to mature, they must be integrated into the routine of the couple's life.

When the natural development of a relationship is blocked at any stage, the cultivation of the factor whose absence has caused the obstruction will allow growth to resume. It is unrealistic to expect that chemistry can be introduced into a loveless couple, but ethics can be. If common goals are drawn out and accentuated in a directionless couple; if commitment is understood to be the barrier by an uncommitted couple, and made; if communication is improved in a dysfunctional marriage; and if consensus is learned and accepted by a competitive couple, the chances of growth resuming in their relationships will be greatly enhanced.

It is important to note that there is *always* room for improvement in relationships. The couple who have learned to communicate still face the challenge of sharing power in their relationship, or coping with subconscious competing goals that may surface in time. At times the commitment in almost any marriage will be shaken by forces internal or external to the relationship, necessitating the commitment's renewal. A couple who had it easy to begin with may be very disheartened when they see problems arising later on; for others, issues only partially resolved from a previous battle may irritably re-emerge for further thought and action. The point is: relationships are a living and therefore constantly growing thing. If they don't grow, they die. A couple who have achieved mastery in the five stages of relationship always have the option of improving their sexual relationship and deepening their spiritual one.

How to select a counsellor

For couples, especially those in a Type D relationship, selecting a helping professional can be very important. If self-help techniques fail, if help from friends and family fails, professional help from a minister, psychiatrist, medical practitioner, psychologist or counsellor can make the difference between separation and divorce, and many more productive years together.

It may seem unscientific, but one of the best ways to get in contact with an effective helping professional is by word of mouth. Knowing someone who has actually been helped when facing a similar relationship problem can be a valuable asset when facing your own. A friend or acquaintance who has been helped by counselling may be willing to answer your questions about it. How many sessions were needed? What was the cost? What was the friend's impression of the counsellor? If you cannot find a referral through an acquaintance, your family medical practitioner may be a good source.

An effective, affordable and available professional is worth the time spent locating him or her. Professional associations, social service agencies or help lines may also provide referrals. When you have chosen a professional helper, remember that actually liking him or her, will increase the likelihood of them helping the relationship's effectiveness. Obviously, if an acute crisis situation exists there is not the time to shop around for a therapist. Convening support from friends, family, or a likely helper or agency to get through the immediate crisis is the necessary step.

Finding a counsellor for longer-term assistance can be taken up when the crisis has subsided.

EXERCISE: WALKING AWAY FROM A FIGHT

It is possible to preprogramme yourself to walk away from a fight before the control point — the point of no return — is reached. This may be set up by intentionally creating an image that will be triggered by a rising conflict. In the calm period of remorse and reflection following a confrontation, imagine taking control of yourself as a fight develops before you lose control. Imagine stopping talking, turning away and leaving. Imagine walking away from the fight — without blame. Imagine being willing to let it go without responding to provocation, to let the other have the last word, to let your ego suffer that little bit from not defending yourself. If anger comes up, let it, without acting on it. Try to make a decision to control your anger instead of letting it control you. Intend to walk away from the next fight as you imagine. Go through this process of creating this mental imagery three or four times. Repeat this process over several days.

It is important for a couple using this technique to not use walking away from a fight as another weapon, but responsibly — for the good of the relationship.

Having done this preparation you may well be able to walk away from the next upset you encounter in your relationship. Whether you succeed at the next opportunity or not, continue to do the mental exercise, including activating your intention. *You must want to be able to walk away from a fight if you are to do it.* If you are not able to exit the third or fourth altercation you encounter, question your intention. Do you really want to avoid fights? Do you really want to improve your relationship? Try to be honest with yourself; examine the possibility that you might believe the relationship is unsalvageable and that you want out. If you do want to try to repair the relationship and the mental exercise still does not work, ask for help from an understanding friend or a professional.

If you are able to control your behaviour in a charged situation, the next step is to look at where the problem lies in your relationship with a view to begin healing it. In light of the additional information provided in this chapter it may be helpful to repeat the exercise at the end of Chapter 3, which involves examining barriers to your relationship.

10 CONSCIOUS SEX

The road of excess leads to the palace of wisdom.

William Blake

Sexuality interjects a potent force into every relationship. A couple's sex life gives them an additional opportunity to express their love. But sex can take a couple to heaven or to hell — causing pleasure or pain, excitement or boredom, bliss or oblivion. Why does such great opportunity carry within it such challenge?

There is a subtext to life, although most people behave as if it does not exist — even if they are aware of it. It is an embarrassing and humbling message if its ramifications are considered. The subtext is simple: no one can control sex; sex controls everyone. This subtext underlies every advertisement using sex — subtly or not so subtly — to market a product, every sex scandal as it hits the newspapers, and every marriage for better or worse.

The hazards inherent in sexual activity are reminders of the fact that sex is resistant to control and restraint. Unwanted pregnancy, sexually transmitted disease, marital infidelity, and compulsive/addictive behaviour patterns are some of the dangers human sexuality regularly delivers. Sex is the great candy store of life; often caution is abandoned in the rush to get at the candy. Experimentation and indulgence in sex are natural, and so is disillusionment thereafter.

Even apart from the more high-profile perils, there can be many complications in the realm of the senses. Sometimes people subconsciously push down their sexual desire out of fear of rejection, failure, other consequences, or out of insecurity or shyness. This is called sexual repression. A sexually repressed person is unaware of it. Others consciously suppress sexual desire for similar or more practical reasons; perhaps, for example, someone may be attracted to his neighbour's wife or daughter and does not know how to handle it. This is known as sexual suppression. Sexual repression is subconscious; sexual suppression is a conscious activity. Neither, however, is a very healthy way to handle sexual energy. Stopping the flow of energy tends to lead to neurosis or illness, or both. Masturbation is another alternative commonly employed to attempt to cope with eros. If masturbation is used to avoid relationship it is not adaptive.

Neither letting sexual energy run wild nor trying to hold it down really works. Entering relationship is the pragmatic way to cope with the compelling but serious realities of sex. Sexual contact is then available, and less likely to get out of control. Channelling sexual energy into a conscious, ethical relationship maximises pleasure while minimising risk.

Sexual energy flowing in a marriage is analogous to electricity in a light bulb: it is contained, so it does not hop about shocking everyone; it is directed to the filament — the energy pathway between husband and wife — and it shines when turned on. In a marriage there is a structure, and within that structure great freedom is available. Confining sexual activity to marriage may seem unpopular, even to some who are married. However, given its uncontrollability, putting sex into an enclosed vessel (a relationship), surrounded by an inert gas (ethics) so that the sparks can truly fly, may not seem a half-bad idea.

Although sexuality is not always fully understood or mastered by couples, it remains central to their lives together. *A functional sexual relationship is essential to a marriage that works.* By applying the concepts that make marriage work to the whole spectrum of their sexual relationship, a couple who wish to have a workable sex life can. In this process some couples will even break through to a new level of sexual expression: conscious sex.

What a couple need to do to have a workable sex life

1. Follow sexual ethics — treat one another as individuals who have the choice to say yes or no.
2. Discuss wishes and expectations about sex.
3. Make a commitment to sexual exclusivity.
4. Communicate: tell each other what the partner needs to know.
5. Take responsibility together for their sexual relationship.

GUILT AND SEXUALITY

All couples face the challenge of maintaining chemistry throughout the course of their relationship. In general, and especially in a couple's sex life, it is essential for them to treat one another with respect to meet this challenge. What kind of sexual relationship can a couple expect to have without treating one another well? In a word, a bad one. It is in a couple's best interests to follow an ethical system in their intimate life. Perhaps it sounds terribly dull to make this explicit. However, those couples who succeed in and out of the bedroom do treat one another well. Injurious, untruthful, dishonest or self-centred behaviour will cause guilt; guilt will suppress sexual energy; suppressed sexual energy will reduce pleasure. Self-interest recommends an ethical approach to sexual relating. It is the first step towards conscious sex.

Guilt is a largely underrated force in sex. The sexual revolution did not erase guilt; however, it did try to deny its power. The slogan of the sexual revolution was, 'If it feels good, do it'. In a few months or years it did not feel so good if harm to someone's feelings was done in the process. In the rush to freedom of the sexual revolution, guilt was buried only to raise its head later. Most people who advocated free love in the 1960s are now married and have children. An important lesson was learned — or rediscovered: sexual injury causes guilt for almost everyone. They may be denied, but the effects of guilt cannot be escaped. Guilt is not just a socially created response, it has deeper roots. *Confusing social guilt with true guilt has led to underrating guilt's importance to sexual relating.*

As Freud pointed out in *Civilisation and Its Discontents,* society has a vested interest in suppressing sexual and aggressive behaviour. Sex is potentially socially disruptive, and society acts to preserve order. As a result, people are *made* to feel guilty about sex by subtle and overt forms of social reproach. In an individual's own estimation, he or she may have done nothing wrong, but is ostracised or punished for nonconforming sexual activity. This is social guilt; its purpose is control. It cannot fully succeed because of sex's uncontrollability, but it does implant guilt. Through social conditioning an individual may be made to feel guilty in spite of having done nothing wrong. This is neurotic guilt. It is a little crazy for anyone to feel guilty if he or she has not erred in his or her own estimation. Neurotic guilt is the individual experience of social guilt. Social guilt was the valid source of rebellion in the sexual revolution. However, to throw off social guilt without replacing it with individual responsibility is throwing the baby out with the bathwater.

True guilt does exist apart from social guilt. Not all guilt is neurotic. Guilt implanted socially is neurotic; however, an individual's own internal sense of guilt is a valid feedback mechanism of what is right and wrong — in or out of the bedroom. It is wrong to try to violate another's power of choice. Someone who does will feel guilty.

Many people are actually more guilty — and consequently less successful — than they are aware because their guilt has been locked in their subconscious mind by psychological defences. An individual denying guilt acts consciously as if the guilt does not exist. Since guilt is unpleasant to experience, we sometimes bar it from consciousness. Psychological *denial* is the will not to believe. An individual denying guilt acts consciously as if the guilt does not exist. *Justification* is another psychological defence mechanism whereby an individual 'makes right' what he or she does, mentally burying guilt. *Rationalisation* is the defence that provides all the good reasons why an act was done in an attempt to psychologically obliterate guilt. If a couple's sex life is not satisfactory, to some degree at least, guilt is probably at play. Although it may have been shut out of awareness, guilt can suffocate pleasure nonetheless.

It is probably not widely accepted that guilt is one of the strongest forces pushing couples apart. Preventing guilt is the best way of protecting a sexual relationship from its negative effects. Living by the principle of non-injury helps to prevent guilt. Practically this means that one partner does not treat his or her counterpart as a thing for the gratification of sexual desire. *The beauty and thrill of sexual pleasure arises between two equal individuals in intimate contact. Treating a partner as an object denies that she or he has choice, breaking the symmetry of equality in the couple.* The essence of injury is denying the other's choice. Rape is the epitome of sexual injury for this reason. *For a couple, following non-injury in sexual contact means treating each other as individuals who have the choice to say yes or no.* If a partner's choice is overridden, guilt will result, and the sexual flow between the couple will be cut down.

Truthfulness and honesty in the realm of sex are also necessary to keep a relationship viable. To lie or hold back the truth concerning sex from a partner is a mistake. Sexual intimacy rests on emotional and verbal, or mental, intimacy. Without truthfulness and honesty how can two individuals get close to one another?

Although it may seem paradoxical, detachment is another element that can improve the overall quality of relating between a couple in their sex life. The compelling nature of sexual desire can short-circuit judgment and restraint, notably so in the first stage of relationship, leading to compulsiveness and hence a brand of sexual activity which may sabotage a relationship's development. If a couple don't feel good about the way they are sexually relating, it will affect the overall relationship. Detaching from the compulsiveness of sexual desire can help. *If you want it, you do not have to have it.*

Fulfilling a desire is not compulsory. A need is something else. If the human body does not have water for a few days it will die; it can last without food for a few days more. Sex is in a different category biologically. However, the sometimes irresistible compulsion to act on sexual desire can obscure this fact. You *can* be sexually aroused and *not* have to do something about it. There is a difference between wanting to have sexual contact and having to act on it. Surrendering to compulsion creates the need for a thing that must be had. It can override other needs within you and block the recognition of signals concerning your partner's and your own emotional and mental state. The imbalance it creates can be a dizzying experience — but remember, in our craving for sexual release and closeness with another we make ourselves vulnerable to emotional pain. Having a degree of sexual detachment, especially in the early stages of a relationship, diminishes the demand for sex and allows for tolerance, understanding and intimate contact to grow naturally — things that sexual compulsiveness often makes impossible.

Sexual energy can be restrained and channelled. The variation in arousal cycles for individuals and between women and men practically means both partners will feel like saying 'Yes' only so often, and inevitably at different times. A rebuffed partner can back off for an hour, a day or a week and put the sexual energy into work or leisure activities. Then, when they both choose, the couple can really let go and enjoy.

SEXUAL GOALS AND EXPECTATIONS

A couple may wish to complete the goals listing procedure (see page 66), applying it to their sexual goals, and share the results with each other. This might not be necessary; however, a couple would do well to discuss frankly what they want and do not want out of their sexual relationship in marriage. Sexual compatibility can be enhanced by considering many of the issues that will arise in a marriage. How frequently does each partner imagine having intercourse? What about pregnancy and birth control? How do they feel about hearing a 'No' when sexually aroused, and how will they cope with it?

Another area that can be targeted by listing goals is unrealistic expectations. What is realistic for one partner may not be for the other. One partner may enjoy having sex standing up in the shower before breakfast, or with olive oil and rubber sheets, the other may not. Taking the attitude that these things will all work out for the best may lead to them working out for the worst. *Discussing wishes and expectations about sex gives a couple a place to start communication about sexual issues with a view to building cooperation on them.*

SEXUAL COMMITMENT

Going over a big waterfall in a row boat with or without the use of the oars is asking for trouble. Entering marriage without sexual commitment is the big waterfall waiting around the bend in relationship. It would be better to know the waterfall's location and row to the riverbank well before the boat is sucked into the current that will carry it over the falls. Amazingly, many couples enter marriage without discussing the issue of sexual exclusivity. They are courting disaster.

Perhaps it is awkward to bring the subject up; perhaps it will be considered a sign of mistrust. Perhaps it will embarrass the real estate agent if the buyer checks the foundation for cracks before purchasing the house. *A wise couple discuss sexual commitment openly before marriage. Sexual commitment means sexual exclusivity.* Those who have reservations, doubts or serious misgivings about making a commitment to exclusivity should try to work through them, discussing the pros and cons. It is better to have a frank discussion before the fact than a frantic one thereafter. In the end, if a couple cannot freely choose to make the commitment, it would probably be better for them not to marry. Sexual commitment is one of the factors that make marriage work; it is a central part of marriage. A couple can have a legal marriage without this pledge, but they will find it extremely difficult to have a marriage in fact in its absence.

Some people want to chase drama in their lives and relationships. It is exciting, glamorous, romantic, tragic, fun. Such people would do better to postpone marriage until they can give up such an approach. They might try reading a book, taking in a movie, going to a play, or auditioning for a part in one. Having a healthy fantasy life in the long run is more practical than acting out drama in relationship. Making it through the stages of a conscious marriage will provide most couples with plenty of drama — of the productive, not the counter-productive, kind.

Sexual commitment is the foundation of trust and security in marriage; it is the basis of an open and loving sexual relationship. It may not remove doubt or jealousy from a relationship, but it will provide an environment to work on them. Sexual commitment is based on choice. Trust and security grow in a marriage when the choice is held to remain faithful, then sexual energy can flow freely between the individuals. Given sexual commitment, a couple can relax into the sexual flow without holding back, without guilt, other mental reservations or fears. Sexual commitment is a powerful contract; it uplifts marriage, adding a higher love to the relationship. With it a marriage will be more likely to bring out the best in a couple.

In the context of a committed marriage, by following ethical principles a couple can allow sexual *unsuppression* to occur. The power of sexual energy under these conditions can intensify to a point not safely attainable and manageable without them. Sexual unsuppression means the release of pent up sexual energy. Unsuppression returns sexual energy that has been repressed or suppressed. For many people, sexual desires will surface that are not socially acceptable. Perhaps the husband will want to go after the neighbour's wife — or husband — or both. If desires such as these arise within the context of a committed marriage, the couple may safely let them. This does not mean you should actually race next door and ring the door bell, leaving clothes scattered between the two houses! In a committed marriage a couple may let the sexual energy intensify, let the sexual fantasies occur and channel it all into their sexual relationship, or into constructive activity when the spouse is not available or willing.

Adherence to ethical principles and sexual commitment are working if unsuppression does take place. It would be foolhardy to abandon them at this juncture. An extension of the guideline for how to land on your feet when you fall in love applies: land on your spouse when you become sexually unsuppressed. Pleasure will intensify to the limit: the pure experience of sexual pleasure will suffuse the sexual contact between the couple. The unsuppressed couple who can let the pleasure be, can find themselves taken to profound mutual orgasm.

Paradoxically, the way to sexual satisfaction is to let go of trying to have pleasure. This also is a form of detachment. *Letting go of compulsion leads to pure experience.* This principle can be utilised by repeatedly approaching orgasm and backing off at the last possible moment. A couple can make quantum leaps in the expression of sexual energy and the experience of sexual abandon in this way. It may take some time, perhaps months or years, but eventually the heights of mutual orgasm can be reached and raised. Again, following an ethical system and keeping the sexual commitment are essential to the success of this procedure. It is a long way down to the bottom of the falls.

COMMUNICATION IN A SEXUAL RELATIONSHIP

A sexually unsuppressed relationship will test a couple's ability to communicate. The whole relationship will intensify, and a new level of communication will be necessary. In order to keep the relationship functioning, the interchange of mental-verbal information between a couple must keep pace with increased sexual intimacy to deal with problems that may surface. The couple may wish to review communication guidelines and sit down together to do Relationship Evolution Dyads (see page 95) if the relationship starts to overheat. It is very important to alternate sexual relating with down-to-earth communication, otherwise a couple's life can become unbalanced. Communication is part of the foundation, including ethical principles and commitment, which makes a healthy sexual relationship an on-going success.

To maintain and improve your sexual relationship, routinely tell your partner what you think he or she should know about yourself as far as sex is concerned. It may be as simple as saying, 'I need more!' or, 'That's hurting'. Perhaps you will need to reveal aspects of yourself you never have before: whatever you think your partner needs to know about you and sex, your sex life together — *whatever* it is that you should tell him or her. A couple may want to do the dyad, 'Tell me what you think you should tell me about our sex life'.

Barriers to communication that remain between a couple will be brought up in the context of an active sex life. Indeed, they cannot be hidden. For example, social guilt with the shame it harbours may restrict communication in the sexual area as social conditioning is confronted by the reality of married life. Perhaps your partner will lock all the doors and pull the curtains one rainy weekend afternoon, disrobe and invite you to do the same — slowly. Perhaps you will be embarrassed and unable to explain why — or be *very* willing but unable to do so.

Another impediment to communication that can not only debilitate a couple's sex life, but endanger the viability of their relationship, is the sexual withhold. Many people feel guilty about some aspect of their past or present sexual behaviour. For example, someone may have been the victim of sexual harassment or abuse and have never shared it with anyone. The problem, as regards the relationship, is not necessarily what happened, but rather the reluctance to tell the other about it.

Someone holding back a communication usually fears the reaction his or her partner might have to it. Perhaps they are afraid their partner will think less of them or reject them if they tell him or her about a past event. If this is the case, they have a sexual withhold. A victim of sexual abuse may fear her partner will believe she did something to provoke being abused, for instance. A sexual withhold — if it is not communicated — can fester and poison a relationship. *Tolerance, understanding and forgiveness are healthy norms to develop within any couple. They create an accepting atmosphere, allowing sexual withholds or other sensitive communications to be expressed.* It is the responsibility of a couple who want effective communication to develop such an atmosphere, and the responsibility of each partner to share his or her sexual withholds for the good of the marriage.

Communication in a sexual relationship is more than just saying, 'No, rub over here', although that may certainly be a part of it. In general, a couple in a conscious marriage grow in their ability to communicate as they grow in their ability to share sexual intimacy. The two are synergistic, each contributing to the other; deeper communication leads to greater sexual intimacy, and increasing intensity in a couple's sex life promotes increased communication. The relationship is then fully and naturally balanced and regulated as it grows and develops.

SEXUAL RESPONSIBILITY TO YOUR MARRIAGE

It may sound like a drag, but it is very important. *In a married couple it is the responsibility of husband and wife to cooperate to maintain an active, healthy sexual relationship.* If sexual activity ceases between a couple the marriage is imperilled. This does not mean that if a couple does not have intercourse for a week their marriage is doomed. The time interval is not what is crucial. It is the couple's intention to overcome problems in their sexual relationship that is important. If a couple give up on their sex life, it is virtually the same as giving up on the marriage. There are innumerable obstacles, many of which have been cited, that can build up and combine to make maintaining sexual contact in a marriage simply seem too hard. A couple may consequently make a silent contract to withdraw from sexual relating. The subject may be avoided, but in most cases the deterioration of the marriage cannot be. A couple must work together when such problems become apparent.

Facing sexual problems is often harder than dealing with problems in other areas of married life. Social guilt, sexual taboos, and closed-mouthed Victorian attitudes can surprisingly appear at these times to undercut a couple's efforts to get on with it or . . .to get it on. The responsibility of coping with sexual problems in a conscious marriage logically follows from a couple's commitment, and would optimally be included in each partner's family duty.

This is not to say, nor is it as simple as saying, either partner should have sex on demand of the other. Everyone has the choice to relate or not, which includes sexual relating. Sex in marriage must be participatory. If a partner is forced to have sex, through subtle manipulation or physical force, that partner is not participating. Mutual choice — *consensus* — must be involved in sexual contact for it to be a psychologically healthy activity. For commitment to endure, for both partners to uphold their choice to preserve the marriage, sexual activity needs to occur between husband and wife or the commitment will eventually be broken. These facts create a dilemma for every married couple: *for a marriage to survive, sexual activity needs to occur, but that sexual activity must be consensual.*

So if she is not in the mood every day for two weeks, her choice should be respected. However, if after a reasonable time her mood does not pass, the couple is obligated to take up the issue. Conversely, if she wants to have intercourse while he is reading the paper, mowing the lawn or doing the dishes, all day long, every day for three weeks running, and he is not quite up to it, some accommodation must be reached. Every married couple will encounter variations of these situations. The problem may be solved simply by asking what is going on, or reaching a resolution may be more time consuming and complicated. Effective communication and cooperation will enable many couples to work out the inevitable problems in their sexual relationships without outside help.

As well as testing the effectiveness of their communication, sexual relations will test a couple's level of cooperation in a marriage. If the dilemma of maintaining a workable sex life precipitates renewed power struggle between a couple, a severe crisis may result. There is no other area — barring outright violence — in which a power struggle may do such lasting damage to a marriage. If both partners cannot give up having their own way in the sexual relationship, cooperation in the maintenance of healthy sexual contact will fall by the wayside. If a couple can actively and lovingly assume their sexual responsibility to the relationship, there is one more reason why it will work.

CONSCIOUS SEX

Sex in marriage certainly does not need to become a duty in the negative connotation of the word. By taking a conscious, growth-oriented approach, sex can provide pleasure and fulfilment to a couple, while enhancing the overall stability, health and effectiveness of their relationship. When a couple keep their conscious attention on their relationship and each other, the quality of their sexual contact will grow and develop.

There is a force that resists sexual restraint — *the ego* — that part of everyone's mind that wants what it wants, and now! By acting on every sexual stirring they feel, a couple can deplete sexual energy and pleasure over the long term. Practising moderate sexual restraint improves the intensity and quality of a couple's sexual contact, and can bring the ego into line. Sexual restraint involves consciously, intentionally refraining from sexual activity. For example, a couple might choose not to touch one another for a month to evaluate the effects of sexual restraint on their sex life. (Or they might decide to settle for two weeks of trial restraint when they find themselves clawing the bark off of the neighbourhood trees.)

Holding back sexual activity does not apply to a honeymoon situation. Every married couple deserve a honeymoon period during which they can enjoy sex to the fullest whenever they choose. Sexual energy will actually increase as sexual unsuppression occurs during the honeymoon.

Starting sexual restraint at the height of unsuppression amplifies its benefits. Moderate restraint cultivates sexual energy, infusing wife and husband with energy and health. Restraint provides intense energy for sexual activity, as well as for creativity. In a conscious marriage, as the couple hold off on sexual activity both spouses will become more and more attractive and desirable to each other. A couple may find it helpful to think of sexual restraint as part of their sexual activity together; an extended preliminary, which may last as long as they wish or can stand it. Loving and wanting each other for a long time makes the eventual contact, a light touch or kiss perhaps, exquisitely pleasurable. The couple themselves are responsible for regulating the period of restraint so that real restraint occurs, but without the energy turning into irritability. Sexual restraint is an aspect of detachment which can add a new dimension and power to a couple's sexual relationship.

When, following a period of intentional restraint, the couple do consent to have sexual contact again, arrangements should be made to allow a full sexual consummation to take place. There should be enough time set aside, at least one-and-a-half or two hours, so that time pressure is not a limitation, and the man has sufficient recovery time to come back in the event of an early orgasm. The time and place should also be arranged to minimise the chance of interruption and maximise the opportunity for having uninhibited contact: doors locked, curtains pulled, phone unplugged, etc. A couple with children may wish to organise for them to play with friends, or schedule other activities for them.

Consummation is quite an appropriate word to describe what happens next. To consummate means to bring to completion, to perfection, to fulfilment. In conscious sex, a couple allow themselves to be caught up, to be consumed by the activity, to let go fully. Having made the preparations, including cultivating restraint, the couple can freely harvest the full pleasure of their sexual experience together. To do so consciously is to do so fully. The technique of conscious sex described at the end of this chapter can help a couple to break through into a deeper realm of contact, love and fulfilment.

In conscious sex true fulfilment is possible. Sexual desire is an indirect experience of the longing for spiritual communion between individuals. Sexual partners parallel spiritual communion in their physical union. In conscious sex, a couple allow deeper contact to become a part of their sexual union, uplifting the relationship. Eros, philos and agape can thereby be integrated in the relationship, adding a depth and meaning beyond that offered by ordinary sexual intercourse. Forcing or resisting this process is counter-productive, but a couple can support it. It will take patience and a willingness to persevere through all the obstacles thrown up by self-centredness and compulsiveness; however, through conscious sex, an ideal absent in most marriages, spiritual communion may be pursued and attained.

Conscious sex in a conscious marriage

Two equal individuals respecting one another's choice to relate sexually can experience the beauty and pleasure of conscious sex. Discussing sexual goals and expectations together enhances a couple's sexual compatibility. Making a sexual commitment elevates a marriage and provides a secure foundation for an open and loving sexual relationship. Tolerance and understanding create an accepting atmosphere in which a couple can share sensitive communications with one another — revealing their fantasies intensifies their flow of sexual energy. Sexual responsibility to the marriage, cooperation with maintaining an active sex life, ensures its viability. Sexual restraint and conscious sex can allow a couple to break through into a deeper realm of sexual contact and spiritual fulfilment.

For conscious sex to be successful it will be helpful for a couple to be healthy so that sexual energy can freely flow. A wholesome diet, exercise, freedom from stress and from alcohol and drugs will support a happy, healthy sex life. An unrested, stuffed, inebriated couple will not be able to enjoy the full experience of sexual pleasure. Alcohol, that great loosener of knickers down through the ages, is not a sexual stimulant. It actually has an anaesthetic effect, being a central nervous system depressant: alcohol deadens the senses. The activity of higher judgment in the cerebral cortex is blocked by alcohol, hence its uninhibiting effects. Some couples rarely or never experience sex without being under the influence of alcohol. Perhaps they should give it a try. It is possible to become as intoxicated by sex as by any drug.

Sexual intimacy can bring beauty, pleasure and joy to a relationship. It is the blossom on the bough of marriage. And for many, having children is the fruit. Sex cannot be controlled, but it can be channelled into relationship — love, pleasure and family. By letting this happen, a couple can enjoy the full benefits of a conscious marriage.

EXERCISE: CONSCIOUS SEX

When engaging in sexual activity, choose to keep your attention on each other. Consciously engaging in sexual contact will increase intimacy, pleasure and satisfaction. As you engage in preliminary sexual activity and then intercourse, do your best to follow these instructions:

- Notice your partner. Notice him or her noticing you. Let yourself really look at your partner. With love, let your gaze go where it will.

- Notice your breathing and your partner's.

- As you touch your partner and your partner touches you (you can alternate this or do it simultaneously), focus your attention on touching and being touched. Really let yourself feel with your hands and your fingers at the point of contact.

- Notice the flow of energy between you and your partner. Let the energy flow without trying to force it. Let go.

If a couple practise conscious sex as described, no one will be treated like a thing. Two individuals will make love.

Conscious orgasm

Another exercise may be added to the method described above to increase your mastery of sexual energy and heighten your pleasure. This exercise should be used only by committed couples who have reached a level of cooperation between them. It may bring up problems if the couple can't work together as a team. If practising the conscious orgasm technique is too frustrating for a couple, the conscious sex instructions may be followed without including it. Perhaps, after some months or years, they might try it again.

There is a control point in sexual activity past which an individual can no longer restrain orgasm. In this exercise, both partners repeatedly approach orgasm but before the control point is passed, stop moving, and intentionally restrain the orgasm. When one partner is approaching orgasm he or she signals the other to stop moving so that orgasm can be restrained. The couple may work out a signal between themselves: a word like 'stop', 'OK, OK' or a pinch is a sufficient signal. When the signal is given both partners stop moving and, to hold back orgasm, contract the musculature in the area of the perineum between the genitals and anus. When the partner who has stopped the movement feels he or she can continue without having an orgasm, activity is resumed. After each partner has approached orgasm one, two or three times (the number is agreed on in advance), the couple may allow orgasm to occur. Either partner may communicate his or her desire to go on and have orgasm at any point; however, to benefit from the effects of the technique it is suggested a couple wait until orgasm has been restrained at least once by each partner. If a partner has an orgasm before this, the couple may continue with the technique if and when both partners agree.

11   ON THE TRAIL OF CONSCIOUS
MARRIAGE

We are not human beings having a spiritual experience. We are

spiritual beings having a human experience.

Pierre Teilhard de Chardin

In the Native American creed, the Great Spirit permeated all of nature. The birds, the sky, the sun and moon, the buffalo, the coyote, the wind and rain were all animated by its metaphysical presence. The lives of the people were guided by signs and portents in nature thought to demonstrate the will of the Great Spirit. In this fashion the people were shown the trail of the true human being to follow through life. Following this trail led to harmony in living.

The materialistic demands of modern living rarely lead to a harmonious life. Modern Western society, clustered in cities, separated from nature, battered by pollutants and stress, has gone a long way from this ideal. The cycle of work and indulgence, work week and weekend often seems to go around and around without leading anywhere. The materialistic ethic of accumulating more and more consumer goods has left a sense of meaninglessness in its wake. The level of alcohol and drug abuse, divorce, adolescent suicide and cultural anomie suggests that something is missing in modern life.

For someone who does not have enough to eat, adequate shelter and warmth, and freedom from danger, life is about physical existence. However, when an individual's physical needs are met, the struggle for physical wellbeing is no longer necessary. Abraham Maslow, the father of humanistic psychology, suggested that individuals then turn toward satisfying 'being-oriented' needs which give life meaning. It is an irony of modern life that when the physical necessities are provided for, so often more material goods are automatically sought, as if happiness will then be assured. Such a philosophy only goes so far. It is nice to have nice things, a sense of security surrounds abundance; however, more is not necessarily better, nor is it what is required. As obvious as this may seem, in the absence of an alternative strategy, the pattern of compulsive materialism appears to dominate modern life.

MEANING THROUGH RELATIONSHIP

Unfortunately, religion, metaphysics, and spirituality are topics that alienate as frequently as enlighten in today's world. The non-physical sciences are often seen to complicate rather than clarify how to live. Integrating spirituality into daily life at the level of relationship is one of the most difficult challenges couples face. But, the uplifting promise of falling inlove can awaken a spiritual longing in a couple. When love deepens in a relationship, the promise of spiritual fulfilment can be kept.

This book has been written to demonstrate that although it is not easy to have a meaningful, or more meaningful, marriage — a conscious marriage — it *is* possible. Depending on an individual's personal history, lifestyle and ability to relate, a workable relationship will be easier or more difficult to achieve. However, those couples who honestly wish to have a go at it may well find the principles and practices in the preceding chapters helpful. A holistic approach to making marriage work also includes the spiritual elements of relationship. In the interests of comprehensiveness, and for those who wish to travel on the trail of conscious marriage, the basics of a spiritual approach to relating follow. This approach is available to everyone; it is not exclusive to a particular denomination or religious orientation.

DIVINE CONTACT IN RELATIONSHIP

In relationship there is always self and other engaging in relating — exchanging thoughts, feelings, and sexual energy. Beneath the layers of personality, the true self is, at heart, divine. The 'other' is the same in nature, but separate. In a relationship, individuals come together to know one another.

Two individuals keeping their attention on one another become conscious of each other. In conscious marriage this practice becomes the foundation of a deeper relationship. Over an extended period of time, if a couple closely attend to one another and their relationship, their sensitivity and intuition will develop. The couple become more attuned to one another, more intimate, more aware of each other and themselves. Given the right conditions they can come into divine contact.

Divine contact is the state of relationship two partners who have accepted one another are in. Each individual becomes aware that at heart the other is divine. They are joined on the ground of their existence, in rapturous communion, by the experience. Erotic love and friendship — eros and philos — arise from and overlay divine contact — agape — when two people fall in love, obscuring or confusing the spiritual connection. However, it is spiritual contact that forms the basis of a loving relationship, and can sustain it through the unavoidable obstacles a couple will encounter. Through divine contact a couple may connect to a spiritual reality that is so often absent in modern life — a reality that many people do not even believe exists.

Two individuals who have fallen in love are in divine contact. This is the experience of agape, divine love. It involves a step beyond consciousness.

If you and your partner sit quietly across from one another, and focus your attention on each other as individuals who have the choice to relate or not, divine contact may occur. Almost anyone trying this technique will notice that in a few seconds or minutes he or she will become distracted. Thoughts of the day, bodily discomfort, nervous smiling or sexual feelings may intrude. It is these normal distractions which routinely divert attention from deeper contact in relationship. When a couple practise this attention exercise, attention is continuously refocused on the partner following a distraction.

In a few minutes, if you and your partner concentrate on each other — the essence of each other — changes may occur. Perhaps the room will seem brighter, your field of vision may seem to expand, and your consciousness may heighten. These are side-effects of deepening contact. You may experience a closeness, love and affinity for your partner. He or she may seem to shine, and the reality of the physical surroundings may pale before the individual-to-individual connection which seems more real. This is the experience of divine contact. How it is experienced will vary from person to person, but certain similarities are universal. A sense of deep regard, reverence and higher love is the signature of divine contact. The relative importance of worldly concerns fades, as a recognition of what truly matters in life is experienced.

The attention exercise is a form of meditation which can be carried into a couple's life. By each individual repeatedly coming back to focus on the other in day-to-day life, meaning, intimacy and a spiritual element may be integrated into a relationship. This is a relating meditation which can also be applied in communication and cooperation, in work and in family life. It is not an esoteric method to be practised alone; it is a meditation of contact between a couple.

A couple practising this technique will find it easier to surmount interpersonal problems, deal with practical concerns, and intuitively know what direction to take in their life together. By focusing their attention on one another, they will find that solutions to problems emerge from the contact. The magic of synergy will build.

HARMONY IN CONSCIOUS MARRIAGE

Such an approach as described in the previous section may sound almost supernatural and, depending on how nature is defined, it indeed might be. The fact remains that a couple maintaining at least a degree of divine contact in their relationship will simply know things they need to know about how to live together. It is a function of heightened awareness. Its effect is comparable to thinking of the person who, moments later, is on the other end of the telephone — which some discount as coincidence. It's the same as knowing what another person is about to say; the same as seeing your future partner for the first time and knowing he or she is the one; the same as having a sick feeling in your stomach when you just know something is wrong with someone you love.

As a result of this increased awareness, over time a marriage will generate its own direction from within, deal with potential problems before they even occur, and generate a degree of harmony that cannot be denied. This is the path of conscious marriage. A Native American looked to the essence of the natural world for guidance; *a couple may look to the essence in one another for guidance and a sense of meaning.*

The meaning created in conscious marriage can serve as the context in which daily life is lived. In a conscious marriage, a couple work out of love for each other and their children. A sense of purpose surrounds a conscious marriage because the relationship is something real. The ordinary grind of daily living is uplifted when a purpose beyond the material world guides life. As the contact between the couple becomes purer, guidance becomes clearer and more evident, and purpose in life more sure.

CONSCIOUS MARRIAGE AND CHILDREN

Conscious marriage creates a meaningful environment in which to have and raise children. So often children in the modern era seem at loose ends. Family cohesion has decreased, disorienting young people. Purpose and direction for children are lacking, leaving them more and more vulnerable to alcohol and drugs, antisocial behaviour and even suicide. A marriage based on true contact between wife and husband can open to include the children.

When parents put their attention on the children as individuals with choice instead of treating them as objects to be moved around, the children benefit. *Conscious parenting involves the choice of the child, instead of overriding it.* Children then are naturally more cooperative and alive. In a family that grows out of a conscious marriage, the parents' sense of purpose and meaning is transmitted to the children, and the best in the children is drawn out through conscious contact. Consequently, these children stand a better chance of discovering who they are, what they want in life and how to achieve it.

The usual purpose of a family is to provide support for children to grow to physical and intellectual maturity. A higher purpose for a family is to nurture children to psychological and spiritual health.

MUTUAL ACCEPTANCE IN CONSCIOUS MARRIAGE

The human family, like any family, has its problems and disagreements, and like any family has to learn to live together and work out differences in the common interest of harmony.

Each individual in the family of humankind is unique, yet everyone shares the commonality of kinship by being members of the same human family. Someone might object by arguing that identical twins are not unique because they both have the identical genetic makeup. Anyone who has known a pair of identical twins could attest to the individuality of each one, despite their genetic identicalness. This suggests that there is more to individuality than genetics, that there is more to an individual than the body.

There is: individuals have the power of choice. Everyone is related by the commonality of having that same choice: to relate or not. This is the great opportunity and challenge of life and relationship. Such a choice creates the potential for relationship, and provides the direction in which life unfolds. To consciously participate in the fulfilment of life in relationship gives meaning to human existence. In this approach, life is seen as the unfolding of relationship, with the choice to relate leading to happiness, fulfilment and meaning; and the choice not to relate leading to isolation.

A couple may choose to erode their relationship or to improve it; a family may choose to live together in harmony or not. The beauty of life is that choice is involved in fulfilling its potential. If life were automatic, it would be meaningless; if people were things without choice, life would have no purpose.

Conscious marriage

On the trail of conscious marriage two individuals consciously make the choice to relate with each other, to go on together on life's path. Two people who fall in love make the choice to relate, two people who have developed common goals and committed their lives to one another hold that choice through time. A couple who weather the storm of establishing effective communication and cooperation between themselves extend their mutual choice to keep their relationship growing. When a child is born, the couple involve the child's choice in their life together. By focusing their attention on one another, a family acknowledges one another's power of choice and a spiritual bond of divine love is included in marriage and family.

Conscious marriage provides a way to reinstate choice in a relationship, and a way to bring a spiritual dimension to life through relationship. The state of relationship that results from this mutual choice is analogous to setting up two mirrors facing one another: a window to the infinite is created. In mathematics this is known as iteration, expansion by repetition. In conscious marriage, this direct individual-to-individual contact is the source of the synergistic power of marriage.

Mutual acceptance points a couple's relationship towards true fulfilment. Instinctive, emotional and mental patterns activate and interact to produce the recognisable stages of a conscious marriage: meeting, courtship, living together, marriage and family. Through a couple's mutual acceptance, the factors that allow for the stages of relationship to be successfully passed spontaneously emerge: chemistry, common goals, commitment, communication and consensus. The result: an effective relationship delivers on the promise of marital synergy; physical fulfilment in the sexual communion produces joy, pleasure and, usually, offspring; emotional fulfilment binds and sustains the union with love; spiritual fulfilment is realised with the individual-to-individual contact of mutual acceptance, divine love.

CONSCIOUS MARRIAGE IN THE TWENTY-FIRST CENTURY

Relationships have suffered long enough from dysfunction. Too many of us, too many of our friends and families, have been caught and dragged under by the destructive forces in relationship because couples have not known what they need to know and what they need to do to keep their relationships growing. They haven't had the blueprint or the tools to build solid marriages.

Relationship offers couples today a great opportunity and a great challenge: a couple moving into the twenty-first century together can take their marriage past the dysfunction of present forms of relationship to a conscious marriage — a new model for marital synergy. If a couple take the appropriate steps at the appropriate times they can confront the obstacles standing in the way of success and solve their problems. Conscious marriage puts this power to understand and improve their relationship in their hands. By consciously facing the challenges of growth, a couple are able to take the necessary actions to fulfil the promise of falling in love.

By staying in contact, by acknowledging one another's power of free choice to relate or not, and by bringing technical knowledge of relating to bear when needed, couples can raise their relationships to a new level of conscious contact, of creative synergy and of marriage itself, to create a true marriage — one that brings meaning and inspiration to their lives together.

The traditional form of marriage has been breaking down and a new, *functional* structure has not replaced it. We need a new model to emerge — one that involves couples consciously, intentionally and actively in the growth of their relationship. Every couple is faced with the choice to adopt such a strategy, or risk being caught in the revolving door of dysfunction. If enough couples take up the conscious approach — and there are many who do want more effective relationships — a transformation of marriage, and society itself, can occur. The consequences of the way couples live their lives will be felt by them, their children and us all. At stake is our own success and happiness — as well as the future of marriage. The new century awaits us, and a new form of marriage is waiting for couples who will take up the opportunity and the challenge.

EXERCISE: ATTENTION DYAD

The purpose of the Attention Dyad is to help a couple increase their ability to keep their attention on one another as individuals with free choice. The exercise is done in the dyad format; that is, with each partner taking turns in keeping their attention on the other while the other monitors.

The monitoring partner gives the instruction, 'Put your attention on me as an individual having choice'. The partner who has received the instruction puts and keeps his or her attention on their partner. The monitoring partner watches to see that he or she does so. When the monitoring partner notices that the working partner's attention has drifted, he or she says, 'OK. What happened?' The working partner then tries to notice what distracted his or her attention, where it is now and/or what his or her internal state is, and reports to the monitoring partner who watches, listens and tries to understand the response. After five minutes the roles reverse.

The Attention Dyad can be done for twenty or forty minutes. When both partners can hold their attention on the other for five minutes without distraction, they may find doing the variations of the dyad suggested below more rewarding. The newly increased ability to attend to the partner can be applied in the life of the couple during communication, sexual contact or other activities.

As mentioned earlier in this chapter, the Attention Dyad can be done without the active monitoring of the partners. Two partners sit across from one another keeping their attention focused on each other as individuals having the choice to relate. (Taken into daily life, the Attention Dyad becomes the relating meditation.)

Couples can apply this same principle to doing another variation of the exercise in a dyad format by intending to accept the other as an individual with the choice to relate or not.

INDEX

Books by The Crossing Press

Clear Mind, Open Heart:
Healing Yourself, Your Relationships, and the Planet
By Eddie and Debbie Shapiro

Numerous real-life stories are interwoven with practical exercises and techniques in this uplifting, inspiring, and deeply sensitive approach to healing through spiritual awareness. Wellness through understanding the bodymind connection helps us find magic and joy in our everday lives.

$16.95 • Paper • 0-89594-917-2

The Language of Dreams
By Patricia Telesco

Patricia Telesco outlines a creative, interactive approach to understanding the dream symbols of our inner life. Interpretations of more than 800 dream symbols incorporate multi-cultural elements with psychological, religious, folk, and historical meanings.

$16.95 • Paper • 0-89594-836-2

On Women Turning Forty: *Coming Into Our Fullness*
By Cathleen Rountree

These candid interviews and beautiful photographs will inspire all women who are navigating through the mid-life passage. The updated look of this bestselling classic makes it the perfect companion to the later decades of Rountree's series on women.

$14.95 • Paper • 0-89594-517-7

Women's Ventures, Women's Visions: *29 Inspiring Stories from Women Who Started Their Own Businesses*
By Shoshana Alexander

Shoshana Alexander presents inspiring profiles of 29 remarkable women who found a way to establish their own enterprises and realize their dreams. Despite their diversity in age, socio-economic class, and ethnic background, they are not that different form all of us who have a desire for financial independence. What distinguishes them is that they have achieved it.

$14.95 • Paper • 0-89594-823-0